Pattern Designing
for
Dressmakers

by Lynn Alexander

Published by   Hobby House Press, Inc.
Grantsville, MD 21536

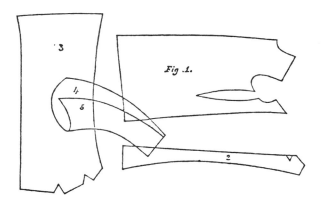

Godey's 1880

Additional copies of this book may be purchased at $14.95 (plus postage and handling) from
HOBBY HOUSE PRESS, INC.
1 Corporate Drive
Grantsville, Maryland 21536
1-800-554-1447
or from your favorite bookstore or dealer.

Printed in the United States of America

ISBN: 0-87588-536-5

Contents

Introduction

1 The Basic Pattern 2

2 Fitting Standards 4

3 Fitting Standards 1860-1930 6

4 Pattern Alteration 9

5 Darts 17

6 Adding Fullness 28

7 Closings, Extensions and Facings 34

8 Yokes 44

9 Bodices 52

10 Collars 62

11 Sleeves 74

12 Skirts 87

13 Equipment 100

14 Completing the Pattern 101

References 102

Basic Pattern for 18" child doll 103

Introduction

Imagine the thrill of making extraordinary clothes from patterns you design yourself. Now, by learning pattern making, you can do just that.

Pattern Designing For Dressmakers is written for dressmakers, stage costumers and doll dressers. It takes the mystery out of designing sewing patterns by demonstrating clearly and simply how to use professional flat pattern making methods.

Three techniques--moving darts, adding fullness, and developing closings, extensions and facings--are the keys to flat pattern designing. The techniques are logical and easy to learn. This book teaches you to master and then combine them to make all sorts of yokes, collars, sleeves, bodices and skirts.

Perhaps you are a dressmaker who wants distinctive, one-of-a-kind garments, without haute couture price tags. If you learn pattern making, you can start with an illustration or mental picture and create whatever you like. You can make new designs, or develop fashion details that give style and variety to patterns you already have.

If you are a stage costumer, the chance of buying the patterns you need is remote, especially if you want historic designs. You must construct authentic looking garments that fit, but do not restrict the actor's movements. Chapters on fitting and alterations help you hone those essential skills. A good working knowledge of professional pattern making methods will enable you to produce successful costumes efficiently.

As an antique doll dresser, you want to costume your dolls as beautifully and correctly as possible. However, you can not always find suitable patterns. Patterns are sold but they may not be the required size or they lack variety and authenticity. With pattern making skills and a good understanding of historic costume, you can design the styles you need.

You can achieve the effect of period clothing with modern pattern making techniques. The outline of the resulting pattern pieces may not necessarily correspond to the shape of the old patterns (which often have contours that are unfamiliar to us). If you have vintage patterns to use as a guide, you can duplicate them in other sizes using the methods presented here.

Hundreds of examples are included in this book to demonstrate how flat pattern making principles are applied. Exquisite fashions from major American women's magazines published between 1870 and 1930 give you solid research information. They will also inspire you with exciting design ideas.

The flat pattern making method taught here is orderly and logical; the concepts are easy to learn. It is also an exact craft, requiring careful concentration, measuring, drawing and cutting. If you enjoy pattern making enough to practice and master the techniques, you open gates to a whole new dimension in dressmaking. You have at your fingertips more design possibilities than you can use in a lifetime of sewing--either for yourself, your children, your actors or your dolls.

I wish to express my appreciation to Bess Ferguson and Jane Farrell of Iowa State University for their encouragement and help with the first edition of this book in 1978, and to my family and friends for their faith and assistance with the revisions.

May you find as much pleasure and satisfaction in making patterns as I do.

Lyn Alexander
1988

Reprinted from Harper's Bazar 1894.

1

1
The Basic Pattern

Clothing patterns are developed in a number of ways--some more accurate than others.

The three major professional methods of pattern making are:

1. DRAFTING--creating a pattern by using body measurements.

2. DRAPING--creating a pattern by molding fabric on the body or dress form.

3. FLAT PATTERN--manipulating a basic pattern to add design details.

Each method is efficient and useful for certain designs. Drafting is easy to use for straight belts, cuffs, ruffles and pleated or gathered skirts. Other patterns are best done by draping or manipulating fabric on the body or form to create drapery, bustles, surplice or cowl necklines, or flowing trains. But, for a wide variety of designs, flat pattern making techniques are the easiest, most accurate and efficient way to develop or change a pattern.

In this book I present elementary flat pattern making methods. Take time to understand and master each step before you try it in your pattern.

To be a successful pattern maker, you should be neat and exact. Carelessness wastes time because you must correct and then re-do it, losing track of the logic of the method, and becoming frustrated. Accuracy is essential for a pattern maker, but especially so for those who are working in small scale. An error of 1/16" in doll size could mean that the garment will not fit, or seams will not match.

In most textbooks, flat pattern work is done by transferring the basic pattern without seam allowances to heavy paper or tag board. This is called the basic, sloper, block, master or foundation pattern. Using simple, logical techniques, it is changed in various ways to develop any number of patterns.

To make pattern development easier, the master pattern has no seam allowances, hems or facings. They are added after the design work is completed.

A basic dress pattern makes a simple five-piece garment with minimum ease and no design details. It has a bodice front and back with high round neckline, long fitted sleeve, and knee-length skirt front and back. Darts mold the dress smoothly to body curves.

To make a master pattern, start with a commercial basic, or simple dress pattern. Press it, and pin it to firm muslin. Transfer all notches, seam, dart, hem and grain lines with dressmaker's carbon and tracing wheel. **Warning: Be sure your muslin is grain perfect, and you mark and cut your pattern accurately.**

Cut out your pattern, baste together, try it on, and fit it. Make alterations, taking care to keep the muslin grain perfect. When the garment fits exactly, take it apart and press it, again keeping the grain accurate. (See page 9.)

Pattern designing is simplified when you start with a perfectly fitting master pattern. You can add design details, but still retain the fit of the original pattern.

Strengthen your master pattern by bonding it to firm, non-stretch, fusible interfacing. To make copies for pattern designing, transfer all the notches and lines to heavy paper with carbon and tracing wheel.

The paper you use for pattern designing must be stiff enough to hold its shape when cut and spliced. Typing paper is good for small patterns. Brown Kraft paper, butcher wrap or blank news print can be used for larger sizes. Tissue paper is not stiff enough to be accurate.

Doll dressmakers can purchase basic patterns, or adapt simple dress patterns to this use. A sample child doll basic pattern is located on page 103.

Photocopy the small basic pattern on the next page to practice pattern making techniques shown in this book.

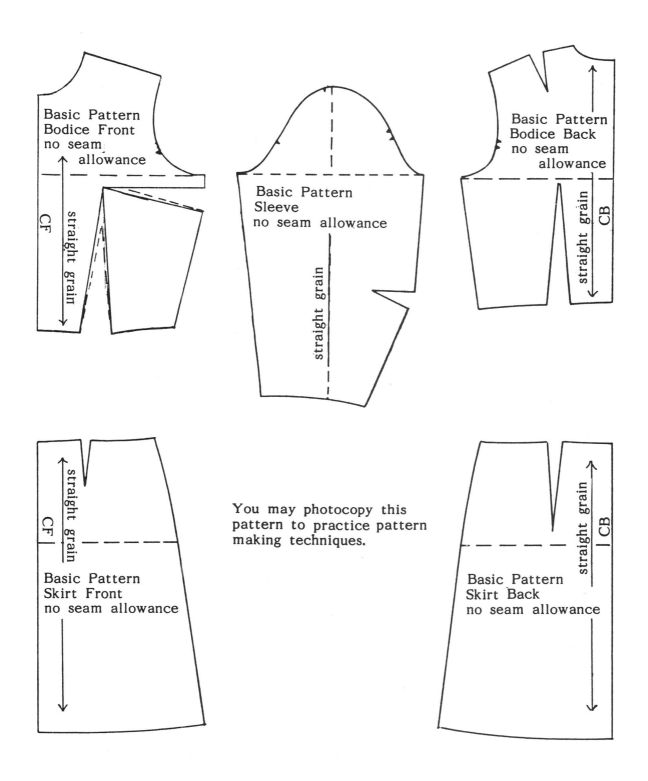

Basic Pattern
Bodice Front
no seam
allowance

CF

straight grain

Basic Pattern
Sleeve
no seam allowance

straight grain

Basic Pattern
Bodice Back
no seam
allowance

straight grain

CB

straight grain

CF

Basic Pattern
Skirt Front
no seam allowance

You may photocopy this
pattern to practice pattern
making techniques.

straight grain

CB

Basic Pattern
Skirt Back
no seam allowance

Fig. 2. A basic dress pattern.

3

2

Fitting Standards

Proper fit, or the lack of it, will make or break your dressmaking, especially in the small scale of dolls' clothes. **Correct fit is more important than design, more important than fabric, and even more important than sewing, if you want to reproduce period costumes.**

If you are familiar with the history of dress, you will consciously or unconsciously assess each garment and decide whether the fit is correct for the period, then you will go on to analyze the costume.

The fitting and altering sections are grouped together because they are interrelated. Here they are directed primarily to basic patterns, but the techniques apply to fitting or designing any garment, or altering any pattern.

Fig. 3. A well-fitted garment.

A concise and useful organization of fitting standards was written by Mabel Erwin in her book <u>Practical Dress Design</u>,[1] first published in 1933. Her five categories are: ease, line, grain, set and balance. These five factors work together, though they are not always equally obvious.

In a simple dress, or a basic pattern good fit will be revealed by:

1. EASE

Ease is the increase in size of a garment beyond actual body measurements. A basic pattern has minimum ease, but should not bind or draw. Garment use influences amount of ease (work or sports clothes need to be more roomy than dress clothes). Age is also a factor (since children grow rapidly, their clothes are rarely tight fitting). Fashion continually decrees changes in ease, and this gives important clues for dating a garment.

2. LINE
a. Basic silhouette seams.

Center front (CF) and center back (CB) are straight vertical lines at the body center front and center back.

Seen in profile, the bodice shoulder and underarm seams and skirt side seam should appear to be in a continuous line from ear-tip to ankle, dividing the front and back of the figure about evenly.

b. Circumference lines.

Circumference lines follow natural body curves. The neckline comfortably hugs the neck. The armhole is straight for a short distance across the shoulder and then is oval following a natural crease where the arm joins the torso. Waist and hemlines of a skirt or short sleeve are parallel to the floor. A long sleeve hem follows the wrist curve.

1. Mabel D. Erwin, <u>Practical Dress Design</u>, New York: The MacMillan Company, 1933, 1964

c. Design lines.

Design lines within the silhouette (pleats, darts, gores, etc.) appear to hang perpendicular to the floor. Curved lines are direct, graceful, and flow smoothly from one pattern piece to another.

3. GRAIN

a. Grain determines how the garment hangs, and changes less than some other fitting standards. In a simple dress CF and CB are on lengthwise grain and perpendicular to the floor.

b. At both hip and bust crosswise grain is horizontal (or parallel to the floor) and perpendicular to CF and CB, as far as the point of the bulge.

c. In sleeves, lengthwise grain hangs straight from the shoulder tip perpendicular to the floor as far as the elbow. Crosswise grain in the sleeve top is parallel to the floor.

d. As design details are added to the basic pattern, grain may be changed to give a variety of fitting and design effects. For instance, sometimes bias is used to make the garment cling to the figure.

4. SET

Smoothness of set is freedom from unwanted wrinkles radiating from a body curve or bulge. If the garment wrinkles because it is too tight, alter it for more ease.

Control excess fabric wrinkles by making darts that radiate in any direction from the bulge point. Darts hold fullness in one area and release it in another to help shape fabric to body curves.

5. BALANCE

Balance in fitting refers to the way the garment rests on the figure. It is anchored by the shoulder seam, which sets evenly on the top of the shoulder. The garment should hang the same distance from the legs front and back and side to side. The sleeve is eased smoothly over the cap, and centered over the arm with approximately the same amount of fullness in back and front.

Balance can be changed from symmetrical to asymmetrical by concentrating fullness in one area or another, as in a bustle or drapery. Balance in fitting and design are closely interrelated.

3
Fitting Standards 1860-1930

1860. In the mid 1800s, sloping shoulders were the ideal, so shoulder seams were moved to the back where they slanted from neckline to armhole. Armholes extended beyond the shoulder points, and were high and tight under the arms. Very tight bodices required princess seaming. Waistlines were usually high, and skirts very full.

Fig. 5. Reprinted from from Harper's Bazar 1884.

Fig. 4. Reprinted from Harper's Bazar 1868.

1880. Fitting standards in the 1880s were similar to the earlier period except that armhole seams were at the shoulder point at the top. The underarm portion of armholes remained high and tight. Princess seaming was still used for a smooth tight fit, but waistlines were now "normal". Sleeves were usually cut in two pieces and had very shallow caps. Skirts were several widths of fabric seamed together, then pleated at the top to fit. The bustle was the most obvious design feature, thus balance in the skirt was asymmetrical.

1890. The biggest change in the 1890s was Leg O' Mutton sleeves, which grew from modest to extreme fullness that required various kinds of inner supports to hold them out. The "Hour-glass" figure with full bust and rounded hips was idealized; requiring a new corset design. Waists were small and waistlines variable. Shoulder seams were still slanted and to the back of the "normal" shoulder. Skirts began to be gored to help eliminate some bulk at the waist. Grain was often matched straight to bias in the side seams (possibly for economy in cutting.)

Fig. 6. Reprinted from Harper's Bazar 1894.

Fig. 7 Vogue 1906

1900. By 1900 Leg O' Mutton sleeves were gone and many sleeve styles from slender to full were used. An "S" curve figure was the ideal, but that ended a few years later. Often the waistline dipped in front, and the bodice bloused over it. Shoulder seams were on top of the shoulder and armholes were at the shoulder point on top, but not so high and tight in the underarm portion as previously. Skirts fit rather close from waist to knees and then flared out in "trumpet" shape. Children's clothing began to have more ease as concern for comfort grew.

7

1920. The ideals of the flapper era and escape from tight corsets were reflected in the very easy fit of clothes in the 1920s. Sleeves were often kimono style, cut in one with the bodice. When sleeves were set-in, the armhole was at the shoulder point on top. Waistlines were almost always low (unless nonexistent). Skirts were slim and sometimes had bias "handkerchief" draperies. Hemlines were above the ankle for women, and above the knee for little girls.

Fig. 8. Reprinted from the Delineator Magazine 1924. Used by permission of the Butterick Company, Inc.

1930. By this time the fitting standards of ease, line, grain, set and balance were pretty much the same as we use today. Shoulder seams followed the shoulder, armholes were neither high nor low and waistlines were "normal", following the indentation between hip and chest. Skirts were

slim and the ideal figure was flat and boyish. Hemlines were variable, though often mid-calf for women and mid-thigh length for girls. These styles can easily be worn today.

Fig. 9. Reprinted from the Delineator Magazine 1930. Used by permission of the Butterick Company, Inc.

This brief analysis of fashion from the viewpoint of fitting standards is meant to increase your awareness of their importance in successful period costuming. Train yourself to observe how clothes fit in the world around you, and in period costumes when you have the opportunity.

Study photographs of dolls in original dress and notice how the fit of their garments reflect the fitting standards of their day. View dolls in competition to see whether the fit of the clothes is appropriate and adequately contributes to the over-all effect.

8

4

Pattern Alteration

Similar principles govern fitting, draping and altering. They are all concerned with manipulating cloth on a form or body, observing the standards of correct fit, making changes or alterations by increasing or decreasing size, and changing darts or circumference lines until the desired fit is obtained.

Fitting standards change with fashion, and must be reflected in period designs. When you make a new pattern from the basic one, these standards should be included as part of the design.

Since careful work is required to develop the exact lines of a pattern, you will do less damage to those lines if you make most of the alterations in the interior of the pattern at or near the body area needing the change.

STEPS TO SOLVE FITTING PROBLEMS

1. Pin your basic pattern to muslin with CF of bodice and skirt on the fold. Add seam allowances (extra wide if you want). Transfer all seam, dart, grain, center front and center back lines with a tracing wheel and dressmaker's carbon paper. Stay-stitch the armhole and neckline and put gathering threads in the sleeve caps. Using the longest stitch setting, sew darts and seams of bodice and skirt. Press. Stitch together at the waist, leaving CB open. Stitch dart and underarm seam of sleeve. Try on. Pin sleeve into place, matching symbols.

2. Study the garment and check each of the five fitting factors (review chapter 2).
   a. EASE. Does the garment pull, gap or draw because it is too small, or sag because it is too large? Do you need to add fabric or remove it?
   b. LINE. Are the basic silhouette seams in proper location at CF, CB, shoulder and side seams? If not, will adding or removing ease solve the problem? Are the circumference lines in proper location? Check the neck and armhole.

Check the length of bodice, skirt and sleeve. Again, do you need to take up or let out in one area or another?
   c. GRAIN. Are CF and CB perpendicular to the floor? Is the crosswise grain at bust and hip horizontal from CF to the bulge? Is the vertical grain line of the sleeve perpendicular to the floor, and is the crosswise grain horizontal?
   d. SET. Are there unwanted wrinkles radiating from a body curve or bulge? Will adding or subtracting ease solve the problem? If not, darts are the solution (as they can be with grain).
   e. BALANCE. Correcting for ease, line, grain and set will result in perfect balance.

3. Pin fit. If the garment is too large, pin in tucks to take up the excess fabric. If it is too small, let out seams and take accurate measurements to determine exactly how much extra fabric is needed and where. If the body is generally symmetrical, then the adjustment is divided among the various pattern pieces; but if one area is unusually prominent or flat, then concentrate the adjustment in that pattern piece. Remember this principle; MAKE THE ADJUSTMENT WHERE IT IS NEEDED!

> Since the outer lines of the pattern have been developed with great care, it is best to make most alterations in the interior of each pattern piece.

4. Baste alterations in the garment, using a ruler to straighten any irregularities you may have made in pinning.

5. Fit the garment again. Make further necessary revisions.

6. When you are satisfied with the fit, copy the alterations in your paper basic pattern. (If you are testing a fashion pattern, it is possible to make alter-

ations in the muslin garment, splice in extra fabric as needed, and then carefully take it apart to use as your finished pattern.)

MAKE THE ALTERATIONS

Alterations can be grouped into a few fundamental categories:

1. Changing darts.

2. Increasing or decreasing size (evenly or in a wedge).

3. Changing seam lines.

When a change is made in one pattern piece, consider the effect this has on adjoining pieces. If one piece is changed, all corresponding parts must be changed so the seams will match. True all seam lines and darts with a ruler or French curve after the changes are made. The following illustrations show samples of alteration principles. Similar alterations can be made in the other pattern parts.

CHANGE DARTS (See "Darts" Chapter 5.)

1. Relocate a dart (Fig. 10).
   Relocate a dart if it is in an incorrect position for the figure. Fitting darts must radiate from the point of the bulge if they are to release their fullness where it is needed (A).
   Relocate a dart if its position is incorrect for the garment design (B).

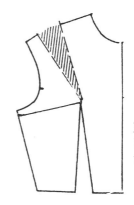

B
Underarm dart moved to shoulder.

2. Increase or decrease dart size (Fig. 11).
   Change dart size when there is adequate ease over the bulge. If there is excessive fabric at the seam, deepen the wide end of the dart. If more length is needed at the seam, decrease the depth of the dart. The larger or more prominent the bulge, the deeper the dart needs to be. (Remember to adjust the adjoining pattern parts to correspond if changes are made in seam length.)
   If the pattern size has been increased or decreased, the darts must be regulated accordingly.

Fig. 11.

Fig. 10.

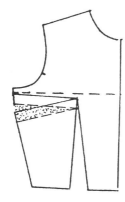

A
Bust dart redrawn to lower position.

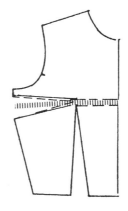

A
Bodice lengthened to give more fabric over large bust. Underarm dart is deepened to match bodice back.

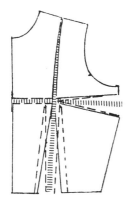

B

If extra length is needed for a large bust, probably extra width is needed as well.

Excessive fullness at the point of a dart is an indication that the dart is too deep for the figure and needs to be made more shallow. In Fig. 12, the excess fabric is removed at the seam line to maintain the waistline circumference.

Fig. 12.

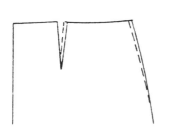

Waist dart made more shallow, and excess fabric is removed at side seam.

Change of dart depth may be used to correct grain if it is necessary to raise or lower the grain in an area.

Dart size may be changed to correct the hang of seam lines. If deepening the waistline darts in only the skirt front pulls the side seams too far forward, then distribute some of the alteration to the back darts to restore balance.

3. Divide a dart.

If a dart is too deep it will release too much fullness at its point. Divide a large dart into two smaller ones to give a smoother effect. Place the two darts on either side of the original larger one, or move part of it to another location (Fig. 13).

Fig. 13.

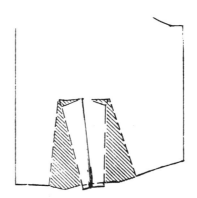

Waist dart divided into two darts.

CHANGE PATTERN SIZE.

INCREASE PATTERN SIZE EVENLY.
Slash and spread to increase width or length (Fig. 14).

Fig. 14.   Increase pattern size evenly.

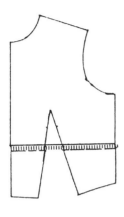
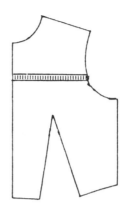
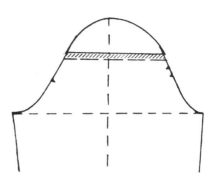

A.   Bodice lengthened below the bust.

B.   Bodice lengthened above the bust. Alter sleeve cap to match.

C.   Lengthen the cap of the sleeve to match a lengthened armhole.

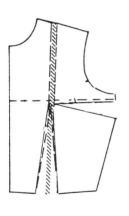
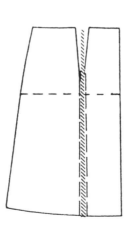
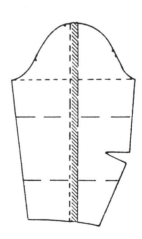

D.   Increase the width of the bodice with a vertical slash and spread. Shoulder is lengthened. Alter bodice back to match.

E.   Increase the width of the skirt. Either make a new dart to restore waistline circumference, or alter bodice to match.

F.   Increase width of sleeve.

Sleeve can be lengthened above and below elbow (dashed lines).

DECREASE PATTERN SIZE EVENLY

Slash and lap to decrease width or length, Fig. 15. (Remember to make the slash WHERE the adjustment is needed.)

Fig. 15. Decrease pattern size evenly.

A. Shorten bodice front above bust. Ease sleeve cap to fit.

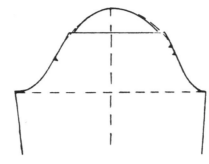

B. Shorten the sleeve cap. In doll's clothes, easing to fit altered armhole will be equally successful.

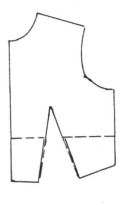

C. Shorten bodice front below bust. Alter bodice back to match.

D. Decrease width of bodice front with a vertical slash. Alter back to fit shoulder.

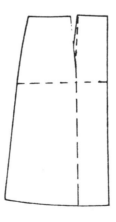

E. Decrease width of skirt with a vertical slash. Redraw dart.

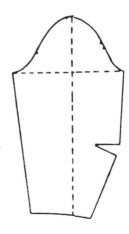

F. Decrease width of sleeve with a vertical slash.

INCREASE PATTERN SIZE IN A WEDGE
   When additional fullness is needed in
one area but not in another, slash and
spread to increase width or length, Fig. 16.

Fig. 16.   Increase pattern size in a wedge.

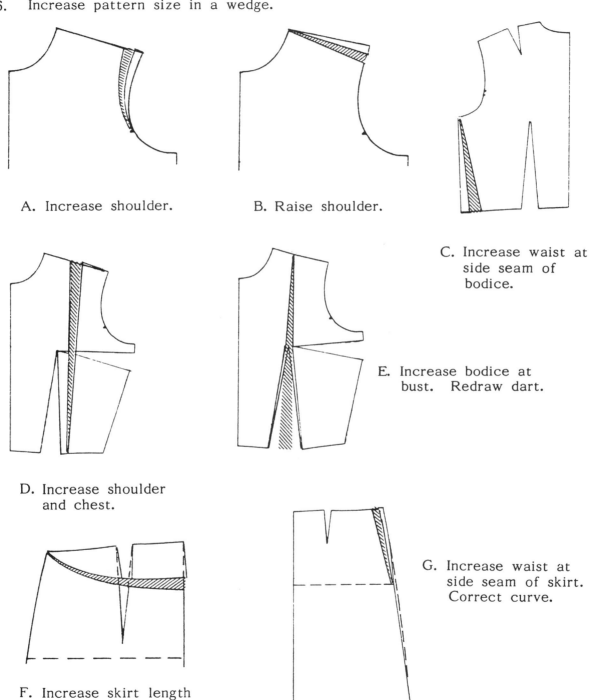

A. Increase shoulder.

B. Raise shoulder.

C. Increase waist at
   side seam of
   bodice.

D. Increase shoulder
   and chest.

E. Increase bodice at
   bust. Redraw dart.

F. Increase skirt length
   at center. Correct
   dart and center line.

G. Increase waist at
   side seam of skirt.
   Correct curve.

DECREASE PATTERN SIZE IN A WEDGE
When excess fullness must be removed
in one area but not in another, slash and
lap to decrease width or length. Fig. 17.

Fig. 17. Decrease pattern size in a wedge.

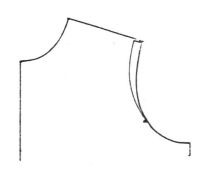

A. Decrease shoulder.

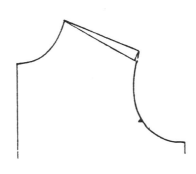

B. Lower shoulder.

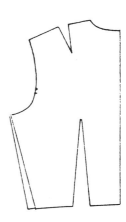

C. Decrease waist at
   side seam of
   bodice.

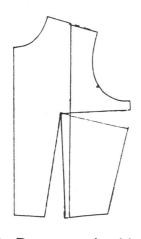

D. Decrease shoulder
   and chest.

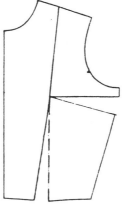

E. Decrease bodice at
   bust. Redraw dart.

F. Decrease skirt length
   at center. Correct
   dart and center line.

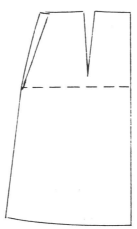

G. Decrease waist at
   side seam of skirt.

While it is possible to make some alterations by changing seam lines, it is rarely successful to use this method to handle major corrections, Fig. 18.

Consider the effect the change will have on the lines of the garment, and on adjoining pattern pieces.

If a seam line, such as the neckline, cannot be corrected in any other way, cut and move it, or redraw it (A).

If the shoulder seam needs changing, but the armhole does not, cut out the armhole area and raise or lower it. Redraw shoulder and side seams in (B and C).

Fig. 18.   Change seam lines.

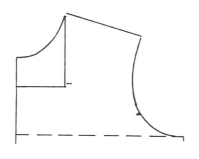 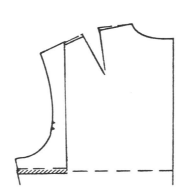 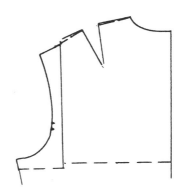

A. Lower neckline.   B. Raise armhole.   C. Lower armhole.

SUMMARY

Retain the pattern's design lines by making internal alterations.

Make an alteration where it is needed.

Make alterations so that the pattern lies flat.

Make edges match.   When an alteration changes the length of an edge that will be seamed to another pattern piece, make a similar alteration in the second piece so that the edges will match exactly.

Maintain the original grain line.

True all seam lines and darts after changes are made. (See page 101.)

5

Darts

Darts or their equivalents are the designer's most useful device to mold flat fabric to the three-dimensional body's wonderful combination of curves. Because they can easily be moved, changed, converted to seam lines, or even added, their manipulation is one of the three elementary categories of flat pattern designing.

A few logical principles govern the function, location, shape and manipulation of darts. With a little practice you can easily master these principles and use them skillfully to develop designs, fit garments and alter patterns.

Practice the examples in this chapter and understand the principles they illustrate. Dart manipulation will be used often in designs in the rest of this book.

FITTING DARTS

Usually when we refer to darts we mean fitting darts--or triangular folds in fabric that are used to shape cloth to body curves. (There is a second kind, decorative darts, which are explained on page 25.)

FUNCTION

In essence, a fitting dart is a controlled wrinkle in the cloth on a dress form or body, and a wrinkle can be a potential but uncontrolled dart.

Fitting darts radiate from the pivot point, or high part of a body curve or bulge, and their wide ends extend to a seam. The larger the bulge, the wider the end of the dart must be.

LOCATION (Fig. 19.)

Fitting darts or their equivalents are used to mold flat fabric smoothly to the seven major body bulges of bust, shoulder, shoulder blade, elbow, abdomen, side hip and derriere.

In the bodice front, all darts radiate from the bust point, and usually their points fall within the area of the bulge, marked by a circle. In the bodice back, the fitting darts have separate pivot points; since one fits the shoulder blade, and the other controls excess fullness at the waistline.

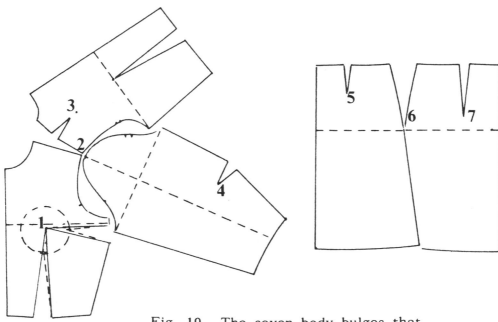

Fig. 19.

Fig. 19. The seven body bulges that require darts.

SHAPE

Darts may be ruler-straight lines or curved in shape. During flat pattern work, straight lines that can be folded or cut into the paper pattern are needed. After the dart moving is finished, the dart can be left straight, or curved for better fitting (Fig. 20). Bodice darts can curve out for a closer fit (a), or in for a smoother curve over the bust (b). In a skirt front, the waistline dart can curve in (c) for a smooth fit over the abdomen.

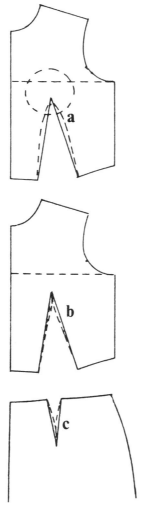

Fig. 20. Shaping dressmaker's darts for a smoother fit.

MANIPULATION OF DARTS

You can easily move, combine, or divide darts, convert them to gathers or conceal them in seam lines. In very loose garments you may choose to eliminate them altogether and let the resulting wrinkles be a part of the design.

18

Fitting darts start at the point of the bulge (the pivot point) and are manipulated from that point (Fig. 21). When they are straight-line and extend to the point of the bulge, they are called designer's darts (a). After the pattern work is completed, they are usually shortened to end within the area of the bulge, and then they are called dressmaker's darts (b). As mentioned earlier, dressmaker's darts can be curved in or out for a smoother fit.

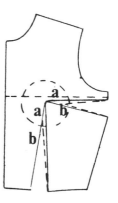

Fig. 21. Designer's darts and dressmaker's darts.

Bodice back shoulder darts are needed to fit the garment to the shoulder blade. Although they are usually small, they are essential, and must not be removed.

Sometimes the shoulder dart is converted to ease, making the back shoulder seam longer than the front. Dots are marked on the pattern to show how it is to be matched for stitching.

If there is a yoke in the bodice back and its line crosses the shoulder pivot point, then the dart is moved to the seam (Fig. 22). If the yoke line crosses above the end of the dart, the remainder of the dart should be eased, thus retaining its fitting function.

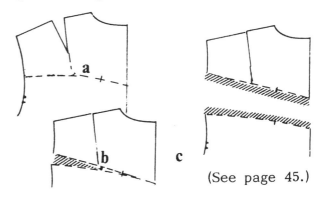

(See page 45.)

Fig. 22. Bodice back yoke.

PRINCIPLES OF MOVING DARTS

You need a thorough understanding of the principles involved in moving darts if you are going to do successful flat pattern work. To master them, practice first with paper, using a circle to eliminate the distraction of a pattern shape.

1. Cut out a circle of paper (5-6" in diameter). Mark a pivot point in the center and draw a dart radiating out from it (Fig. 23, a).

2. Draw a line for the new dart, and continue the line to the pivot point (b). It is easier while the pattern is still flat, but can be done later.

3. Close the original dart by folding or cutting on one line and matching it to the other. Pin or tape the dart closed (c). The circle is now cone shaped and a bulge has been created. Note that a shallow dart will produce a small bulge while a deep dart will cause a larger bulge. Remember: The deeper the dart, the greater the bulge.

4. Cut along the new line to the pivot point and let the pattern flatten out. The space left from spreading the slash is now the new dart. Fill this space with fresh paper (d).

Fig. 23. Moving a dart.

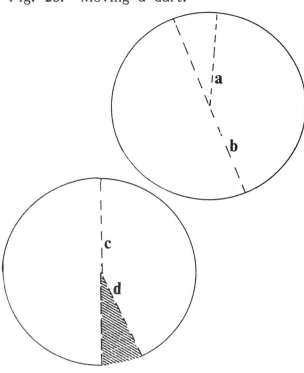

Fig. 24. Dividing a dart.

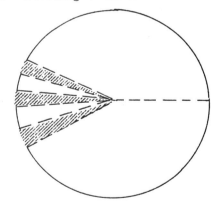

Fig. 25. Incorporating darts in a seam.

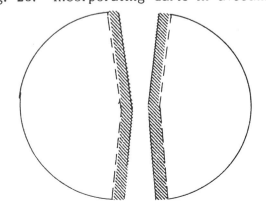

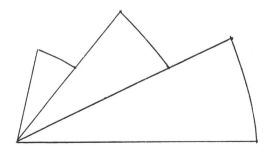

Fig. 26. Long darts seem larger than short ones.

As you experiment you discover that:

a. You can move the dart to any position around the circle.

b. You keep the size of the dart the same.

c. You can divide the dart into more than one new dart. Each new dart is a segment of the original, and the sum of all of them is the same as the original (Fig. 24). You do not always need to stitch the dart closed. Dart equivalents such as ease, tucks, pleats or gathers can control fullness at the outer edge.

d. You can incorporate a dart, or darts, into a seam by cutting the circle in two and adding seam allowance to the dart lines. In Fig. 25, the dart was divided into two darts, and then the pattern was cut apart.

e. Since a dart is a segment of a circle, a longer dart will appear to be larger than a smaller one, even when the degree of angle is the same (Fig. 26).

Fig. 27. Dart equivalents.

1897
Gathers.

Shoulder dart moved to yoke seam.

1899

elbow eased

Shoulder tucks.

1910

Shoulder tucks.
1917

Gathers at yoke.

Shoulder gathers.
1925

Underarm gathers.

All fashion illustrations from <u>Delineator</u> <u>Magazine.</u> Used by permission of Butterick Co. Inc.

20

The three methods for manipulating darts are SLASH, PIVOT and REDRAWING.

SLASH METHOD OF MOVING A DART

1. Begin with a paper basic pattern without seam allowances.

2. Extend the dressmaker's darts to be designer's darts (Fig. 28 A, a).

3. Draw in the new dart, which may radiate in any direction from the pivot point (b).

4. Close the basic dart by cutting or folding, meeting front line to back line. Pin or tape closed, creating a bulge in the pattern (B).

5. Cut along the new dart line to the pivot point. Allow pattern to flatten and legs of new dart to spread. The space left by spreading the slash is now the new dart (C).

6. Fill in the open area of the new dart by taping to fresh paper.

7. Shorten to form dressmaker's dart (C, a). Fold the dart shut, with the fold pointing toward CF, and cut the shape of the wide end (b).

Since this is such a wide dart, it would be better to divide it into three or more darts, or convert it to gathers (D).

Fig. 28. A.

B.

C.

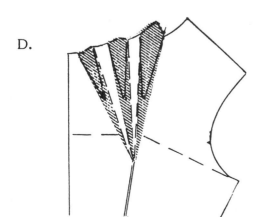

D.

PIVOT METHOD OF MOVING A DART

1. Make a copy of the basic pattern in heavy paper, cut out on the dart lines.

2. Mark the seam line location of the new dart (Fig. 29 A, a). On a fresh sheet of paper, start to trace around the pattern from this point at the shoulder, and continue on around to the first leg of the dart to be moved.

3. Anchor the pivot point with a pin (C, c), and pivot the pattern until the dart to be moved is closed (d). Continue to trace around the pattern to (e). Draw lines on the pattern you have traced from (a) and (e) to the pivot point. The gap which has formed is the new dart.

4. Draw lines for the designer's dart, and shorten to be a dressmaker's dart (Fig. 30).

5. Fold in the new dressmaker's dart to cut shape of wide end. On the wrong side, vertical darts fold toward the center, and horizontal darts fold down. This dart is shown as a dart tuck, that is, not stitched to a point.

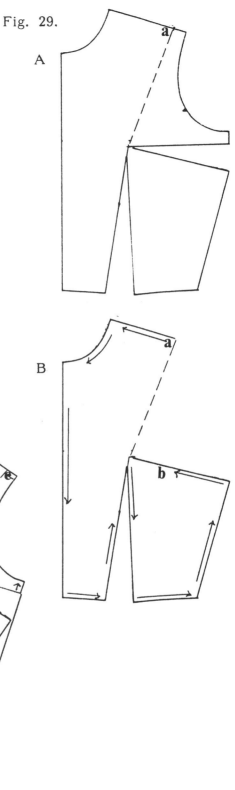

Fig. 29.

A

B

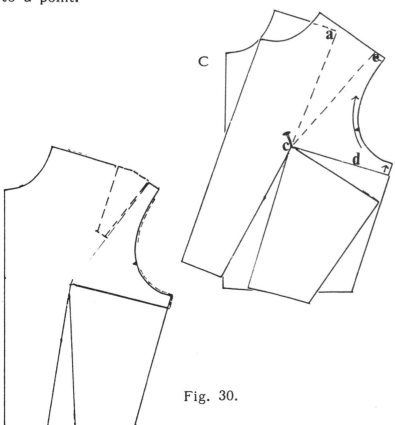

C

Fig. 30.

22

REDRAWING TO MOVE A DART

This method may be used when the dart needs to be moved only slightly.

1. Make a paper copy of the dart. Erase or mark out original dart lines. (Fig. 31).

2. Move the dart to a better position and trace around the paper copy. If a new pivot point is needed to improve fit, position the dart in relation to this new pivot point.

3. Fold in the new dart and recut the seam at the wide end of the dart. Add paper, if necessary, to provide for reshaping the end of the dart.

Fig. 31.
Redrawing a dart.

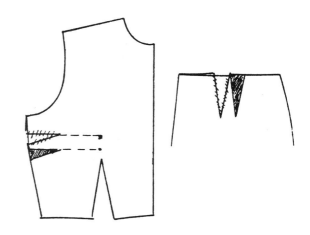

Examples of how to move darts.

A new dart can be converted to gathers or divided into several dart tucks that are stitched only part way (Fig. 32).

Fig. 32.

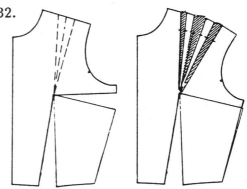

In Fig. 33, the darts are concentrated at the center front waistline, and are converted into three dart tucks on each side. Since these tucks do not radiate from the pivot point, make a horizontal slash from the end to the two center darts to release fullness from the pivot point. Indicate ends of the dart tucks with cross marks on the pattern. Fold dart tucks closed to cut waistline.

Delineator 1897.

Fig. 33.

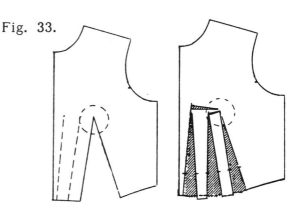

23

To convert darts to gathers, combine all bodice front darts into a single large dart. Mark out the dart. Redraw waist stitching line adding length and curve. Indicate gathering line (Fig. 34).

Fig. 34.

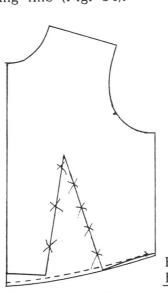

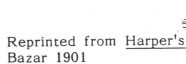
Reprinted from Harper's Bazar 1901

SUMMARY

Fitting darts or their equivalents are needed to fit flat fabric to body curves.

The larger or more pronounced the curve, the wider the dart that is necessary.

A dart can radiate in any direction from the pivot point of the bulge. Its wide end extends to a seam.

Darts can be moved, combined, divided, converted to equivalents or concealed in seam lines without changing the fit or size of the garment.

Darts can be moved by slashing and spreading, pivoting the pattern or redrawing the dart in a new location.

Delineator 1911. Used by permission of Butterick Co., Inc.

Fig. 35.

DECORATIVE DARTS

Fitting darts, radiating from the point of a bulge, fit flat fabric to body curves. Decorative darts are added to the pattern by the slash and spread method, and do no fitting. Sometimes they do not cross or end at the point of the bulge.

Decorative darts need to be kept narrow to avoid releasing too much ease into the pattern. They can be made deeper if they include part of a fitting dart.

Slash to, but not through, the seam line. When seam allowance is present, clip through it to just meet the slash at the seam line.

Try to make the open end of a slash at right angles to the seam.

When a slash enters a seam line, it can cause a distortion in the seam, which will need to be corrected to a smooth curve. A slash directed to a corner will cause less seam distortion.

To shape the wide end of the dart, cut along the seam line with the dart closed.

Fig. 36.

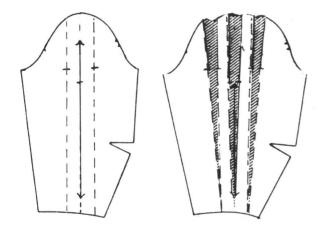

Dart tucks are indicated here. That is, they are not stitched to a point. Gathers, shirring or smocking could also be used.

Fig. 37.

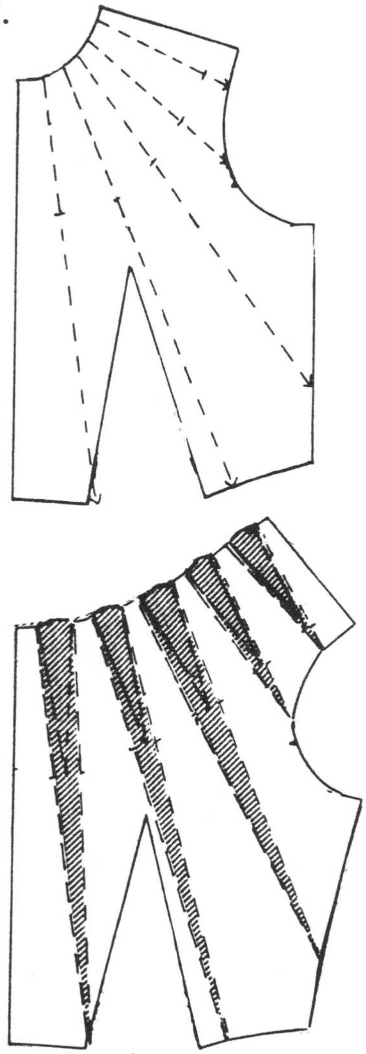

Steps in adding decorative darts:

1. Draw the design on the paper basic pattern.

2. Slash and spread the pattern and tape to fresh paper.

3. Draw the stitching lines for the new darts.

4. Reshape the wide end of the dart by closing the dart and cutting along the seam line.

5. Redraw seam line entered by the slash, if necessary. Convert it to a smooth curve.

1924

1921

1924

1894

1920

1920

1920

1920

Fig. 38. Darts and dart equivalents.
All fashion illustrations from
Delineator Magazine. Used by permission
of Butterick Co., Inc.

26

Delineator 1924

Delineator 1922

Delineator 1922

Delineator 1922

Delineator 1930

Fig. 39. Dart equivalents

Illustrations used by permission
of the Butterick Co., Inc.

6
Adding Fullness

Adding fullness to create style is the second of three elementary categories of techniques used in flat pattern making.

Design fullness such as gathers, tucks, pleats, flare or drapery is added to the basic pattern. It is done by slashing and spreading the paper pattern where you want the fullness. The amount added is determined by the design.

Fullness is added in an <u>even</u> amount by cutting the pattern completely apart and spreading it so that the cut edges are parallel (Fig. 44).

Flare is obtained by slashing and spreading the pattern in an <u>uneven</u> amount. Sometimes you cut to, but not through the opposite seam line and pivot the pattern parts open (Fig. 43). If seam allowance happens to be present on your pattern, then make a clip from the edge of the seam allowance to almost join the slash (Fig. 40). Otherwise, you will add extra length to the seam line.

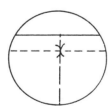

Fig. 40.

When more fullness is needed, cut the pattern completely apart and spread it an uneven amount (Fig. 52).

If the slash crosses or encloses a fitting dart, then the added fullness is not only decorative, but contributes to the fit of the garment as well (Fig. 42).

Work on a suitable surface such as corrugated cardboard, or an ironing board, and stab-pin the pattern pieces to the fresh paper (Fig. 41). When the pieces are arranged to suit you, tape them securely to the paper.

GATHERS

Several methods are used alone or in combination to develop gathers. In each instance, the new seam line will be curved, because gathers need length as well as width. Do preliminary designing in the paper pattern, and make corrections during the garment fitting. Mark the limits of the gathers with a symbol to show where they are to begin and end, and also mark the adjoining seam to match. Do not design gathers too close to the shoulder or neck or they will not hang properly.

1. Fitting darts can be converted to gathers that serve the same function as the dart. They follow all the principles of darts, and are directed to the pivot point of the bulge. They do not increase the size of the pattern (Fig. 41).

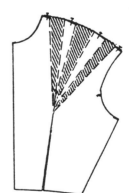

Fig. 41.

2. A dart can be incorporated into gathers by planning one of the slashes to cross the pivot point of the dart (Fig. 42, a).

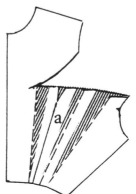

Fig. 42.

3. Gathers can be added the same as for decorative darts (page 25). The pattern is slashed to but not through the opposite seam line and spread the desired amount (Fig. 43).

Fig. 43.

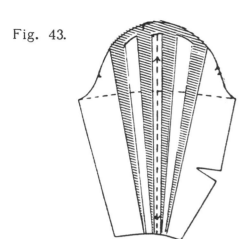

4. Full-length gathered fullness can be added by cutting the pattern apart and spreading the entire length of the slash (Fig. 44). Draw a horizontal guide line on the pattern before slashing. Match to a corresponding line drawn on a fresh sheet of paper. This will keep all the pattern parts aligned correctly (a).

Increase the length at top and bottom of this sleeve to make those edges puff out (b). These are tentative lines and must be tested in cloth and perfected for the best effect.

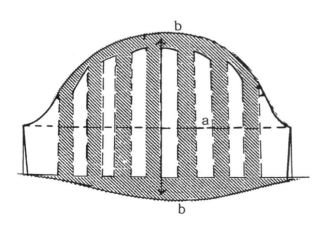

Fig. 44.

Fig. 45.

Delineator 1899

Harper's Bazar 1881

1882

Fig. 46.

ESTIMATING FULLNESS

Ease: add less than 1/2 original measure.
Minimum fullness: add 1 1/2 times original measure.
Moderate fullness: add 2 times original measure.
Very full: add 3 times original measure.

TUCKS

Small parallel tucks can be made in fabric before it is cut by the pattern. Be sure the tucks are accurately spaced, stitched and pressed before placing the pattern on it to be cut (Fig. 47).

Fig. 47.

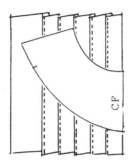

Wider tucks are developed in the paper pattern by the slash and spread method. Each tuck must be measured with a ruler and drawn accurately. Or draw them on squared paper and tape them to the pattern. Draw a horizontal guide line and match to a corresponding line drawn on fresh paper. Slash and spread the pattern, making each tuck perfectly even and twice as wide as the depth of the tuck. Fold the tucks closed before adding seam allowance and cutting the edge. Mark fold line of each tuck and the line it meets, the stitching line and direction of the fold (Fig. 48).

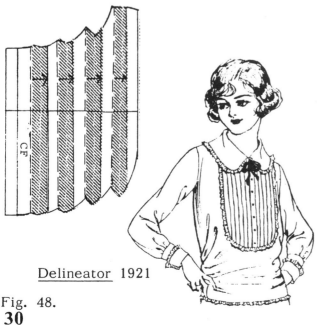

Delineator 1921

Fig. 48.

30

Tucks can be used in separate small areas such as yokes, pockets or collars as shown. They can also release fullness into the remainder of the pattern piece; such as sleeve, bodice front or back, or skirt. For this sleeve, straighten the underarm seam and redraw the hem to allow for gathers (Fig. 49).

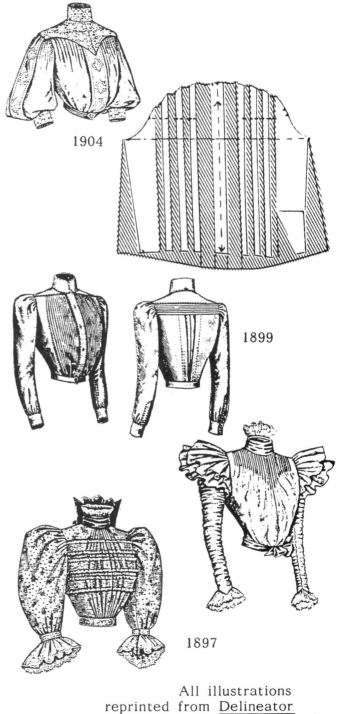

1904

1899

1897

Fig. 49.

All illustrations reprinted from <u>Delineator Magazine</u> by permission of the Butterick Co., Inc.

PLEATS

Pleats are developed in a paper pattern by the same method as tucks, except they are usually deeper and left unstitched or stitched only partly. They will hang better if the fold line follows the heavier grain of the cloth (usually the lengthwise grain).

Pleats can be parallel (the same width from top to bottom) or graduated in width.

Plan pleats by folding them in paper. This helps you visualize the proportions, and shows how much extra fullness must be added to the pattern.

If it is necessary to seam pleats together, cut the pattern apart on an inner fold line and add seam allowance to each piece.

PARALLEL PLEATS
Pleated to fit the hips:
1. Make a copy of the waist dart, then mark out the original dart (Fig. 51).
2. Draw the lines for the pleats an even width apart (a), and a horizontal guide line (b).
3. Draw a corresponding guide line on a fresh sheet of paper (c).
4. Slash and spread the pattern and pin it into position on fresh paper. Measure each pleat accurately. Tape to hold.
5. Divide the dart so a portion is on each pleat (d).
6. Fold pleats on the pleat line up to the dart ends, then fold along the dart lines. Pleats can be top-stitched to the hip line in the finished skirt.
7. Fold the pleats closed to add seam allowance and cut waistline edge.

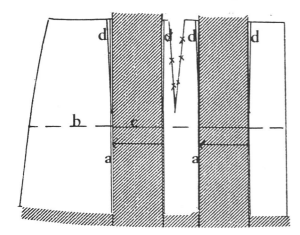

Fig. 51. Parallel pleats.

Parallel pleats can also be fitted to the waist measure if they are not stitched down. They will look better if there is not an excessive difference in measurement between waist and hip.

NON-PARALLEL PLEATS
Non-parallel pleats are graduated in width and often used in gored skirts.
1. Draw line for the pleat, or pleats, and mark notches across it on the pattern (Fig. 52, a).
2. Design and fold in the pleat (b) in fresh paper. This may be a single knife pleat as illustrated, or multiple pleats. Work them out carefully and accurately in paper.
3. Cut skirt apart on pleat line, and pin into position on folded-in pleat.
4. Cut off excess paper while pleat is folded closed.
5. Make seams in the pattern if folds become so bias the pleats will not hang well, or multiple pleats make the pattern too wide for the fabric. Cut pleat apart on the inner fold (c), add seam allowance and make a seam there.

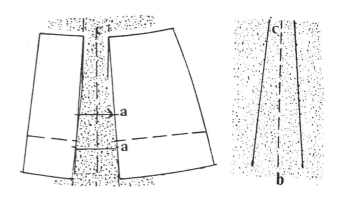

Fig. 52.
Non-parallel pleats.

Reprinted from
Harper's Bazar 1871

FLARE

Flare, or circular fullness is developed by cutting the pattern where flare is desired, slashing to but not through the opposite seam. Similar procedures have been described earlier. (See "Decorative Darts", page 25.)

Slash where you want the flare (Fig. 53). This makes the opposite seam line more curved. The curve that results from slashing and spreading controls the location of the flare and must be carefully preserved. Several slashes will distribute the flare, resulting in a smooth curve (A), while a single slash where a large flare or fold is desired will cause an angle to develop (B).

Use this principle in fitting garments: shift flare from one position to another by changing the curve of a seam.

Adding flare changes the grain line so the effects of bias become more noticeable. Bias collapses in soft fabrics and flares out in stiff ones. A design can be tentatively made in the pattern, but must be tried and corrected in the finished garment's fabric, or in cloth that behaves in a similar manner.

Fig. 53.

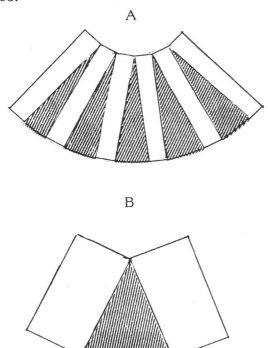

A

B

Fig. 54.

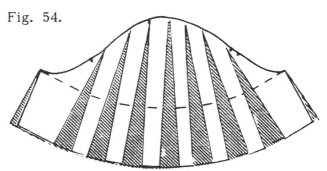

Add flare to a sleeve.

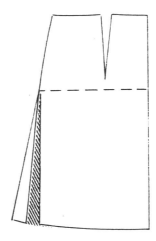

Add flare to the side seam of a skirt.

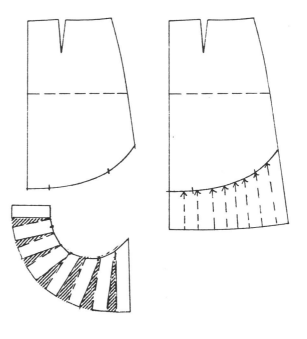

Add flare to a skirt flounce.

DRAPERY

Drapery folds can be horizontal, vertical, diagonal or curved. They are developed in a paper pattern by adapting the techniques used for adding fullness. Draw the design lines on the pattern, then slash and spread to add desired amount of fullness (Fig. 55).

Test pattern in fabric on the figure, experimenting with the folds to determine the best use of grain, bias, and the nature of the cloth being used. Bias will give a softer drape than straight grain and may be used to good effect on the center seam. Soft fabrics such as jersey, chiffon, velvet and crepe drape beautifully. Do not skimp, but make the folds deep enough to be effective.

Fig. 55. Neckline drapery.

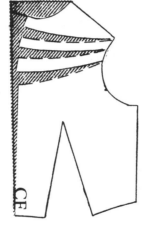

Moderate amount of drape.

Fig. 56. Deep cowl drapery.

Underarm dart is incorporated in drape.

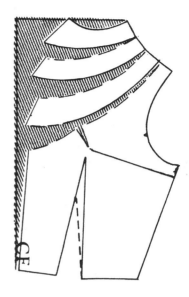

If CF is to be cut on a fold, the neckline must intersect the fold at right angles.

SUMMARY

Design fullness is developed in a pattern by slashing and spreading.

Slash <u>where</u> the fullness is wanted.

For tucks, pleats or full length gathers, the pattern is slashed and spread along the entire length.

Full length gathers require added length as well as width. More length causes puffiness to develop.

For decorative darts, flare or drapery, slash to but not through the opposite seam. If seam allowance is present on the pattern, clip through it to just meet the end of the slash at the seam line.

The curve that develops from slashing and spreading the pattern controls the location of the flare. It must be carefully preserved.

7
Closings, Extensions and Facings

Developing closings, extensions and facings is the third major category of techniques used in flat pattern making. In most cases the manipulation is done at an edge; such as center front, center back, neckline, waist, or hem of sleeve, bodice or skirt. The three are considered together. Although an extension is not always chosen to be the location of the closing, a closing is usually extended to provide for adequate lap. A facing is needed to finish and support the edge.

A successful pattern maker knows design principles and understands garment construction. These skills are especially necessary when she is planning and developing closings, extensions and facings.

ART PRINCIPLES
Space permits us only a brief summary of art principles here. There are many books on art in clothing. A few are listed in the bibliography.

Balance is a sense of stability or equalibrium in a design whether it is symmetrical or asymmetrical.

Proportion is the relation of the size of the structural parts to the whole. The ratio of 2 to 3 is accepted as a standard of fine proportion, although the designer is not limited to that ratio.

Scale is the relation of the size of the parts to each other and to the entire design. Good proportion and scale are harmony of size that is neither monotonous nor overpowering.

Emphasis is pleasing when there is one major area of interest, with all other areas subordinate. Classic clothing designs usually have their emphasis near the face; since few people are dramatic enough to compete with emphasis placed elsewhere. Unless your artistic sense is highly developed, keep your designs simple, but not boring.

Rhythm is pleasing transition that gives continuity to a design. The eye starts with the primary emphasis, moves easily from one unit to another and returns to the beginning. The design is neither static and dull, nor confusingly busy.

Lines (silhouette and interior), color, dark and light, texture, fabric and trim are all components of design.

Sketch your design in a whole front copy of the basic pattern to help you visualize the total effect. You will usually start with the bodice front since it is of primary importance in emphasizing the face.

Avoid gimmicks and overly dramatic effects that few can wear. Transitional curves and conservative proportions are more wearable. Notice that the Erté design in Fig. 57, is shown on a very stark and dramatic model.

Reprinted from
Harper's Bazar 1916

Fig. 57

34

Develop your understanding of art principles in relation to clothing; and your appreciation for good, pleasing and harmonious designs. Recognize the commonplace and the overly fanciful and steer a middle course.

Keep all parts of the design unified by a certain amount of repetition, but introduce enough variety for interest.

Remember that clothes should enhance but not dominate the wearer.

CONSTRUCTION
The successful pattern maker also needs to know how to sew; to understand how the garment will go together and what facings, extensions and hems are required. Skill in construction will help you plan workable patterns.

CLOSINGS
Study illustrations to determine where the garment is opened, and how it closes. Dolls require larger openings than humans because usually their heads are proportionally larger and their bodies are less flexible.

If openings are decorative as well as functional, it enhances the design. Learn to appreciate the variety of ways clothes can be opened and closed.

Buttons can be ordinary or artistic. When there is a long row, separation into groups makes them more interesting (Fig. 58).

Plan uneven numbers of buttons. Three are better than four, unless a belt buckle joins them as a fifth partner (Fig. 59).

Fig. 59. Ladies' Home Journal 1919

Use large buttons sparingly (Fig. 60).

Ladies' Home Journal 1923

Fig. 60.

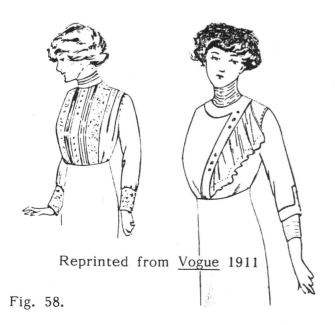

Reprinted from Vogue 1911

Fig. 58.

Tiny buttons can be closely spaced to stand together as a unit (Fig. 61).

Reprinted from Harpers' Bazar 1921.

Fig. 61.

Avoid sprinkling buttons (or any design detail, for that matter) helter skelter. Give them a purpose and let them function. (Fig. 62.)

Delineator 1885. Used by permission of the Butterick Co., Inc.

Fig. 62.

Reprinted from Harper's Bazar 1892.

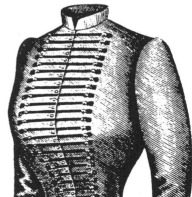

Delineator 1885. Used by permission of the Butterick Co., Inc.

Fig. 63. A plethora of buttons.

Besides buttons, you can also use frogs, cords, chains, loops, lacings, zippers, flaps or ties as visible closures.

Delineator 1885

Delineator 1885

Delineator 1888

Harper's Bazar 1885

Harper's Bazar 1901

Delineator 1920

Delineator 1911

Fig. 64.   All illustrations used with permission.

Buttonholes can be utilitarian or decorative (Fig. 65).

Fig. 65.

Ladies' Home Journal 1910

Openings are concealed by using hooks, snaps, or zippers under flaps.

It also helps to know something about common closures for various historical periods. Hooks and eyes were used in the 1800's, and were hidden under flaps. Buttons in a fly have a special method of construction; and when they are concealed, require an extra layer of fabric in the fly (Fig. 66).

Fall-front trousers have extensions stitched to the pants back (Fig. 67).

Baby dresses in the early 1900s had back plackets made like Fig. 68.

Fig. 66.

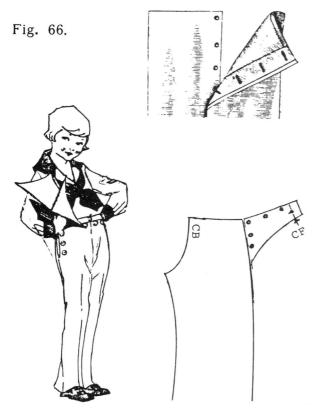

Fig. 67.
<u>Ladies' Home Journal</u> 1919

PLACKET
1. Slash CB to ●, and again across bottom.
2. Fold on fold line 1, then 2. Sew.
3. Meet fold line 2 to CB, forming pleat.
4. Fold on fold lines 3 and 4. Sew. Lap over first tuck. Stitch bottom to hold pleat.

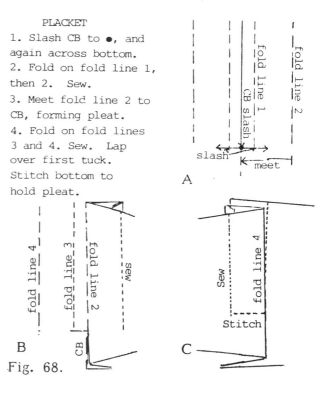

Fig. 68.

EXTENSIONS

The simplest extensions are made by an even width addition, with the facing joined by a fold. Fold on the fold line to cut shape of neckline and waist (Fig. 69).

Fig. 69.

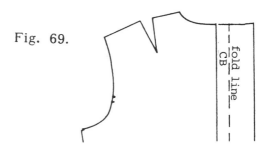

In Fig. 70, the front facing can be straight or combined with the neck facing (a).

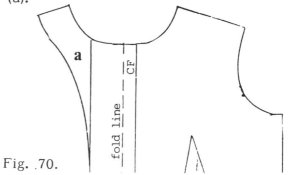

Fig. 70.

A skirt could have a full length extension, or partial placket (Fig. 71, a).

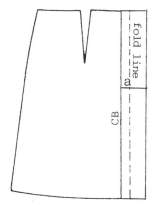

Fig. 71.

The same principle of folding on the fold line before cutting hems in tapered or flared pieces was also used earlier for shaping the ends of darts, tucks and pleats. The dotted lines in Fig. 72, show how a fitted sleeve continues to taper. If the sleeve hem is not shaped to fit at the underarm seam, the too-small hem will cause the sleeve to pucker. The reverse is true when you turn up the hem of a flared skirt. You must remove flare at the seam line to take some fullness out of the hem.

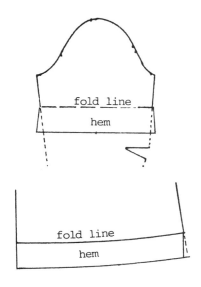

Fig. 72.

When a simple extension is made to the center line and the closing is symmetrical, then both sides of the garment front

or back are cut using the same pattern piece. Simple double-breasted closings are made in this way (Fig. 73). Be sure the facing is sufficiently wide to cover the extension.

1930   1929

Fig. 73.   Delineator Magazine
Used by permission of
The Butterick Co., Inc.

When you see an asymmetric design, picture in your mind how the pattern is cut. Is it a double-breasted or surplice style where both sides are cut alike, or does the under lap need come only part way as in Fig. 74?

Delineator 1921

Fig. 74.

39

DOUBLE-BREASTED CLOSING

1. Use a pattern for the entire bodice front. Draw the closing line. The dotted line shows how the left side will lap under the right side (Fig. 75).
2. Cut the pattern in two on the closing line. For this design the left bodice front can be discarded (L).
3. Make a facing by tracing the cut edge, shoulder and waist. Measure it the desired width, mark notches and add seam allowance. The facing grain is the same as that of the bodice unless there is a special reason.
4. The back facing follows the back neckline in shape and grain, and is the same width as the front at the shoulder. Mark notches where they join.

ASYMMETRIC CLOSING WITH PATTERN FOR RIGHT AND LEFT SIDES
(Sometimes called a "Russian Dress".)

1. Begin with a whole front pattern. Draw closing line and mark notches (Fig. 76).
2. Draw left side grain line parallel to CF.
3. Cut the pattern in two on the closing line.
4. Add underlay extension to the left side (a). For a doll, (b) may be a cut edge and not finished.
5. Make facing for right side. In this instance the neck facing has been included. It is pictured wrong side up to show clearly how it fits the bodice. It would be reversed for cutting.
6. Extend hem and add flare. Complete the pattern. (See page 101.)

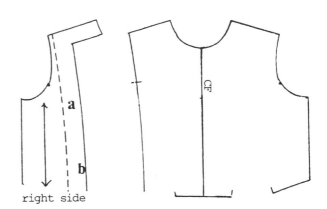

right side

Ladies Home Journal 1900

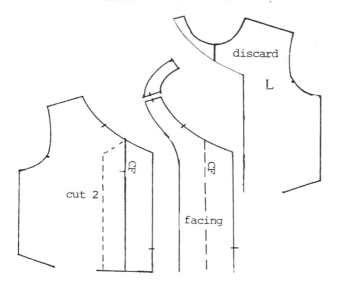

Fig. 75.

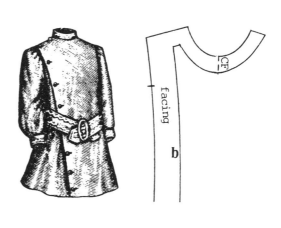

Fig. 76.   Designer 1901

40

FACINGS

A curved edge usually needs a facing as a finish and to support the edge. Facings are duplicates of the edges being faced (Fig. 77).

Shaped facings can be on the wrong side and invisible as illustrated above, or on the right side where they contribute to the design (Fig. 79). In that case, construct them to be a trifle bigger than the garment; so that they will not pucker.

Fig. 77. Delineator 1920. Used by permission of the Butterick Co., Inc.

Fig. 79. Vogue 1910

Facings remain hidden from view if constructed to be slightly smaller than the garment. Slip the facing a bit beyond the edge of the garment and pin. Stitch, measuring the seam allowance from garment edge (Fig. 78). This technique is used when making collars, or whenever one layer must be concealed. Under-stitching is used in human clothes to hold facings in place, but this is difficult to do in tiny dolls' clothes.

Great variety is found in designs for closings, extensions and facings. Some are fanciful and elaborate, but their flat pattern development follows the basic techniques explained here.

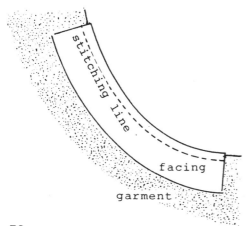

Fig. 78.

Delineator 1923.
Used by permission

Fig. 80.

41

1921

1911

1924

1922

1922

Fig. 81. All illustrations reprinted from Delineator Magazine by the permission of the Butterick Co., Inc.

Delineator 1921

Delineator 1921

Delineator 1920

Delineator 1899

Ladies' Home Journal 1910

Fig. 82. All illustrations used with permission.

8
Yokes

Yokes are made in all shapes and sizes; symmetrical or asymmetrical. They can be purely decorative, completely functional, or both. In the best designs, creative decoration enhances functional use.

Yokes divide areas of a garment into smaller units, and they can be found in any pattern piece. Make them by slashing the pattern apart along a design line, and adding seam allowance to both cut edges (Fig 83).

Fig. 83.

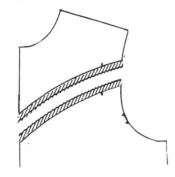

Yoke shapes are limited by what it is possible to sew. A successful designer uses her knowledge of construction to create workable patterns that do not tax the dressmaker's skills.

FUNCTION

Decorative yokes add interest to a garment. To be pleasing they should be artistic in design, conforming to the art principles introduced on page 34.

Yokes will have maximum impact if they are cut from contrasting color, unusual fabric, or are attached by something other than a plain seam.

Fig. 84. Contrasting color yoke.

Delineator 1924

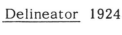

Fig. 85. A yoke cut from tucked fabric.

Reprinted from
Harper's Bazar 1894.

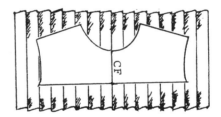

Fig. 86. A yoke cut from lace or rows of insertion, applied on top of blouse and edged with lace.

Delineator 1902. Used by permission of the the Butterick Co., Inc.

Fig. 87. Stripes emphasize a yoke.

Delineator 1888

Yokes can control fullness either from a dart or when fullness is added.

Fig. 88.

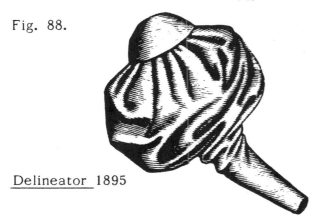

Delineator 1895

Yokes can help in fitting the garment when a dart is concealed in the seam.

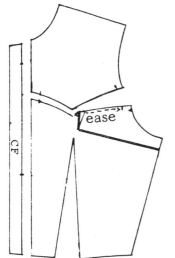

Fig. 89.

Delineator 1901

Bodice back yoke.

Bodice back shoulder darts seem small, yet they are essential in fitting a garment to the shoulder blades. They must be retained in pattern designing, and can be moved, converted to a seam or eased at the shoulder. When a yoke in the bodice back intersects the pivot point of the dart, the dart can be moved to the seam. If it comes below the pivot point, the dart must remain, or be converted to ease. If the yoke line comes above the pivot point, that part of the dart below the line can be eased to fit.

1. Locate pivot point for dart. Draw yoke line (Fig. 90 A, a).
2. Measure the dart width at the shoulder, and mark this distance below line (a) at the armhole. Draw line (b) from pivot point to armhole. Mark notches.
3. Close shoulder dart (B). Cut pattern apart.
4. For this design, slash and spread pattern for pleats.

Fig. 90.

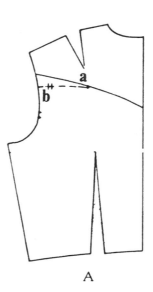

Delineator 1901

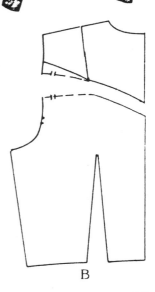

A   B

45

Yokes can also provide the location for an opening or an extension such as a pocket.

Fig. 91. A yoke with an opening.

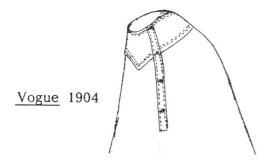

Vogue 1904

Fig. 92. A yoke with a pocket.

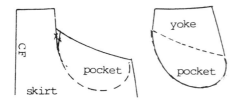

CONSTRUCTION

When you are designing or making patterns, think through each step and use logical construction methods. The dressmaker will appreciate your consideration in easing her task.

Plan the construction of the yoke. Decide what kind of seam will be used to attach it, which direction the seam allowance will be pressed, and whether facings or extensions are needed.

A seam will be less bulky if fullness is not folded back on itself. A plain yoke joined to a gathered body will usually have the seam allowance pressed toward the yoke (Fig. 93).

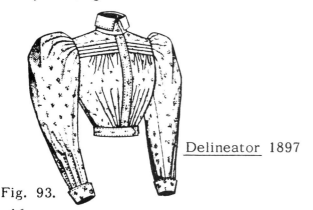

Delineator 1897

Fig. 93.

46

In Fig. 85, the skirt is pleated, and the yoke is tucked. Pressing the seam allowance toward the yoke will make pleats in the skirt hang better.

Stay-stitch seam lines of both yoke and body to help you reassemble the parts exactly. This is especially necessary with shaped yokes and curved seams. In human clothes, stay-stitching is done 1/16" away from the stitching line, in the seam allowance. In small dolls' clothes, you must stay-stitch exactly on the seam line, then pin and baste carefully for a precise match.

Notches and clips are used to keep seams flat. Notch outside curves that will turn inward, and clip inside curves that turn outward. Trim or clip corners before turning (Fig. 94).

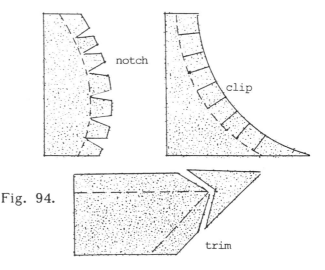

Fig. 94.

Top-stitching is decorative, strengthens the seam, and holds the layers in place.

The inset yoke in Fig. 95 A, could be stitched to the blouse in a plain seam. The seam allowance of the blouse must be clipped, so that it can be pressed away from the yoke. Top-stitching controls the layers.

In human size the blouse edge would be faced. Baste yoke to the blouse on the seam line, then remove bastings after top-stitching is done. This gives more depth and importance to the inset yoke (B).

Notice that this yoke is not only decorative, but is also the location of a laced neck opening.

Yokes can be attached with slot seams, fagoting or other fancy stitches.

The edge of yokes can be decorative. In Fig. 97 A, blanket-stitch is used; in B, piping; while C, has top-stitching and the fullness is smocked.

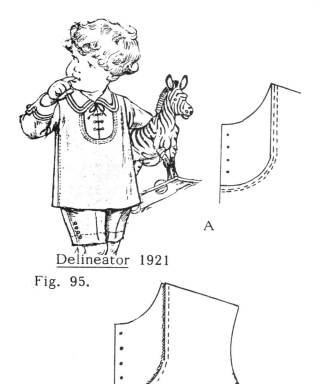

Delineator 1921

Fig. 95.

A

Delineator 1919

Yokes can be on top of the garment. In Fig. 96 A, the yoke seam holds the ruffle, and all seam allowances are pressed toward the yoke.

Delineator 1895

All illustrations from Delineator Magazine used by permission of the Butterick Co., Inc.

Fig. 96.

Delineator 1921

Fig. 97.

Some designs can be interpreted in different ways. The yoke in Fig. 98, is developed in two steps. First, draw the design line for the lower edge of the yoke on the bodice front (A). Cut lower bodice apart and add fullness and length. Then draw the design lines for front piece and its attached facing on the yoke (B). Cut apart and add seam allowance to all edges.

Another possibility is to design the yoke (Fig. 99 A), and treat the upper piece as a plastron (B). This solution is easier to construct, and the plastron gives a more interesting three dimensional effect. The buttons are both decorative and functional.

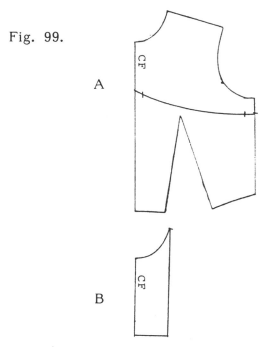

Fig. 99.

Yokes which continue from one pattern piece to another can sometimes have the linking seam eliminated. ·This changes the grain in one piece (Fig. 100).

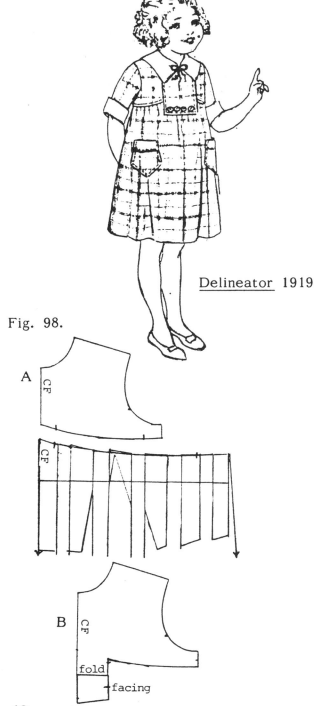

Delineator 1919

Fig. 98.

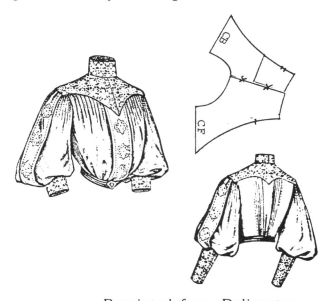

Fig. 100.

Reprinted from Delineator Magazine 1904 by permission of the Butterick Co., Inc.

48

LOCATION

Yokes can be located anywhere the design calls for them. They can be in the bodice front or back, sleeve, skirt front or back, in pants, or in pockets.

Fig. 101, shows two designs with yokes above pleated skirts.

Delineator 1904

Fig. 101.

In Fig. 102, the skirt yoke (B) is asymmetrical, but the pattern work would be similar. Use a whole front and back pattern.

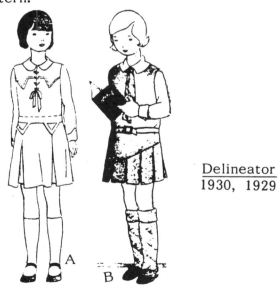

Delineator 1930, 1929

All illustrations from *Delineator* Magazine used by permission of the Butterick Co., Inc.

Fig. 102.

Gathers or flare could also join a skirt yoke as in Fig. 103.

Fig. 103. Delineator 1929

Yokes in petticoats and drawers eliminate gathers over the hips and help to control waistline bulk. Therefore, they are very useful in dolls' clothes (Fig. 104).

Fig. 104. Girl's drawers. Delineator 1888.

STEPS FOR MAKING A YOKE

1. Draw design line on pattern. Lines should flow smoothly from one pattern piece to another.
2. Mark notches.
3. Cut pattern apart.
4. Move dart when appropriate.
5. Redraw seam line to a gentle curve if an angle has developed.
6. Add seam allowance to both pieces.
7. Establish grain line, and complete pattern.

1923

1916

1923

1911

1916

1921

1921

1921

All illustrations reprinted from Delineator
Magazine by the permission of the
Butterick Co., Inc.

Fig. 105. Yokes.

50

Harper's Bazar 1919
3-year-old boy

Harper's Bazar 1906
3-year-old boy

Delineator 1920

Harper's Bazar
1916

Harper's Bazar 1919

Harper's Bazar 1916

Delineator 1919

Fig. 106.   Yokes.   All illustrations reprinted with permission.

The bodice is often the focal point of design in a costume. It is usually the first part of the pattern to be developed, and all other pieces are subordinated to it.

NECKLINE FULLNESS

Review "Moving The Basic Dart", page 22. Darts, tucks, shirring, smocking or gathers can control the wide ends of darts. Darts, tucks and pleats need accurate measurement, while gathers may be drawn freehand.

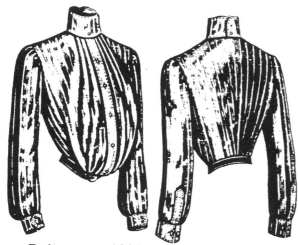

Delineator 1901

In the shirtwaist design (Fig. 107), neck fullness is controlled by tucks which appear to be on straight grain. Therefore, they are made by adding fullness evenly.

1. Start with all bust darts moved to the waist.
2. Draw line for front band and mark notches.
3. Draw tucks parallel with CF.
4. Slash and spread pattern an even amount, carefully measuring each tuck with a ruler. Tape to fresh paper.
5. Fold tucks toward CF and pin closed. Cut along neckline.
6. Make pattern for front band. See page 59.
7. Lower waistline so it droops over belt as illustrated. Indicate gathers across front, including darts.
8. Add seam allowance and complete the pattern.

Delineator 1895

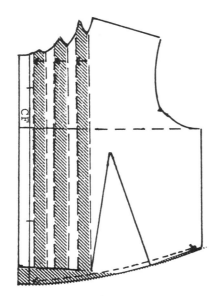

Fig. 107.

Fig. 108.

Fig. 109.

Delineator 1925

TUCKS, PLEATS OR GATHERS
Review "Adding Fullness", page 30.
1.   Combine underarm and waistline darts. Draw yoke line (Fig. 110).
2.   Draw lines for pleats.
3.   Draw horizontal guide line and corresponding line on fresh paper.
4.   Cut on yoke line.
5.   Starting from the center, slash and spread each section, making all pleats equal in width.
6.   Fold pleats closed and cut top seam line. Extend lower edge.
7.   Complete the pattern.

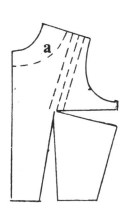

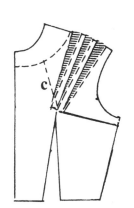

DART MOVED TO SHOULDER
1.   Draw new neckline (Fig. 109, a).
2.   Draw lines for shoulder gathers.
Avoid getting too close to the armhole area or gathers will fall off shoulder. Shirring or a shoulder yoke can be used to stabilize the gathers (b).
3.   Close underarm dart.
4.   Slash on gather lines and move dart.
5.   Tape to fresh paper. Draw a new curved shoulder, adding length for gathers. (For darts: draw them in, cut pattern on dart lines and continue as explained before.)
6.   Cut new neckline. If neck gaps during fitting, take up shoulder a small amount at neckline to remove excess, or pin in a small dart and move to shoulder (c).
NOTE: This design could be done just as well using your princess or shirtwaist sloper, developed on pages 56 to 59.

Delineator 1920

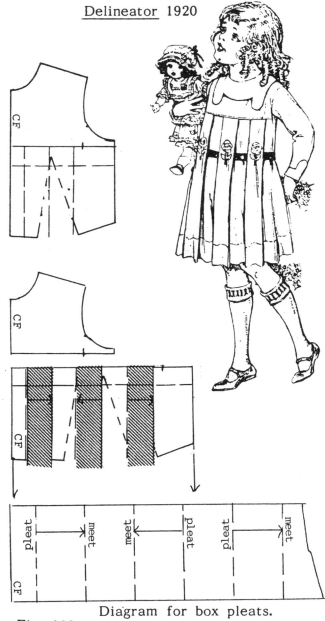

Diagram for box pleats.
Fig. 110.

DECORATIVE DART WITH FULLNESS

"Review Decorative Darts", page 25.

1. Draw decorative dart. Mark notches. Draw lines for slashes to add fullness (Fig. 111).
2. Draw horizontal guide line and corresponding line on a large sheet of fresh paper.
3. Extend and close underarm dart.
4. Slash and spread pattern, moving dart and adding fullness. Redraw upper curve, adding length for gathers. Notice that the seam allowance near point (a) becomes very narrow and the gathers cannot extend beyond (b).
5. Extend hem to dress length.
6. Complete the pattern.

Delineator 1924

Delineator 1923

Fig. 112.

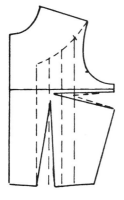

Delineator 1925

Fig. 111.
Decorative dart
with fullness.

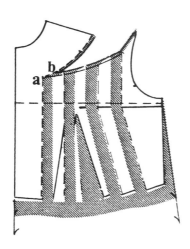

Delineator 1923

54

Fig. 113.

Harper's Bazar 1888

ASYMMETRIC SIDE OPENING

Review "Extensions", pages 39 and 40.

This dress is a bit more complicated than those explained earlier, but uses the same pattern making principles. It will, of course, be designed differently on the right and left sides of the bodice front.

1. Begin with a whole front bodice pattern. Draw line for asymmetric opening (Fig. 113 A, a). Cut pattern apart and discard left side. Extend the right side at the waist, longer at CF than at side seams. Convert dart to gathers.
2. Make facing (b). Mark notches, and draw grain line to match CF.
3. Draw lines for left side shoulder tucks on fresh whole front pattern (B). Move part of waistline dart to tucks, making tuck nearest neck larger (a).
4. Cut pattern apart at tuck (b), and add fullness so tucks are equal in size.
5. Close tucks and cut along shoulder.
6. Drop waistline to match pattern (A). Convert darts to gathers.
7. Add seam allowance and complete the pattern. Extend bodice back to match.

Ladies' Home Journal 1919

Fig. 114. Asymmetric side openings.

PRINCESS SEAM

The princess seam, which changes darts to a seam, is often found in designs with a smooth tight fit. It is a popular style that returns to fashion favor again and again. Vertical lines seem to elongate and slenderize a person, and gentle curves are becoming to a mature feminine figure.

Princess seams can be used in both the bodice front and back. When all or part of the skirt is joined to the bodice, you have the basis for a jacket or a princess dress. This can be used as a sloper or master pattern for many other designs.

A princess seam converts shoulder and waistline darts to a seam. It is usually designed to fall over the bust point, or slightly closer to center front. Other variations are shown in Figs. 116 and 120.

As usual, you must test your design in muslin to fine-tune the fit and make needed corrections. The tighter the fit, the more necessary it is to try the pattern on the figure.

Fig. 115. Princess seam in bodice front.

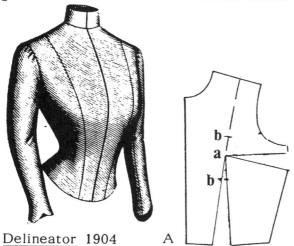

Delineator 1904   A

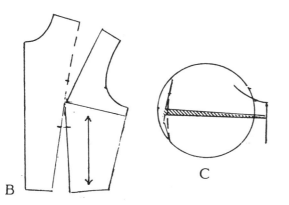

B   C

PRINCESS SEAM IN BODICE FRONT

1. Draw seam line from shoulder to waist, intersecting the bust point (Fig. 115 A, a).
2. Mark notches above and below bust point (b).
3. Cut pattern apart (B), cutting along both sides of waist dart. Close underarm dart.
4. Improve curve at pivot point.
5. If more ease is needed over bust, slash along line of underarm dart to side seam and spread pattern a small amount (enlargement C). Ease to front, matching notches.
6. Establish grain line in side front either parallel with CF or centered in side panel.
7. Add seam allowance to cut edges and other edges, if necessary. Complete the pattern.

Fig. 116.

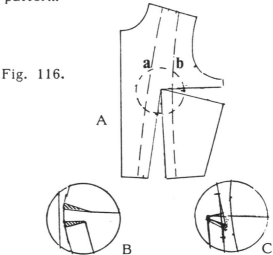

A

B   C

If the princess seam comes closer to CF than the pivot point (Fig. 116 A, a), slash from the seam line to the points of both underarm and waistline and allow pattern to spread. The extra fullness will be eased into the seam (enlargement B).

If the seam comes closer to the side seam (b), then slash from the seam to the point of the waistline dart and spread pattern. Open point of underarm dart. Ease side front to fit front between notches, (enlargement C). Redraw the seam line to a smoother curve on both sides of the seam. This will remove a small amount of ease over the bust. Test the pattern in muslin to be sure it is correct.

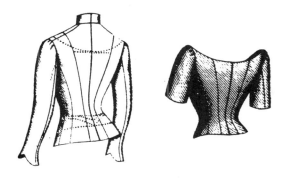

Delineator 1904

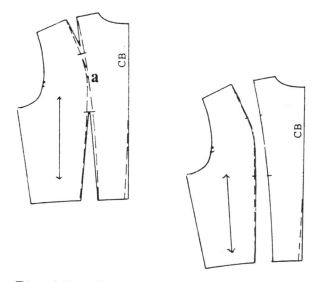

Fig. 117. Princess seam in bodice back.

PRINCESS SEAM IN BODICE BACK

1. Mark pivot point for shoulder dart (Fig. 117, a). Usually there are separate pivot points for the shoulder and waist darts in the bodice back, but for a princess seam, use only one at the shoulder.
2. Sketch princess seam line if it coincides with the darts. (If not, close the darts first, draw seam and slash from seam to the dart point to release fullness and flatten pattern.) Mark notches. Draw grain line in side back parallel with CB.
3. Cut pattern apart on seam line. Redraw a smoother curve.
4. If your design calls for a center back seam, draw in a smooth curve.
5. Complete the pattern.

You can see that ease has been removed from the pattern, and this explains why testing the fit in fabric is essential.

PRINCESS SEAM FROM ARMHOLE

1. Draw new seam line, mark notches (Fig. 118 A).
2. Extend shoulder dart to pivot point and close.
3. Cut pattern apart, cutting on both sides of waistline dart.
4. Make several small slashes to pivot point of shoulder dart to flatten pattern (B). Fullness will be eased into seam between notches.
5. Smooth curves.
6. Add seam allowance to cut edges, and complete the pattern.

A similar bodice front pattern is shown in Fig. 119.

Fig. 118. Princess seam from armhole.

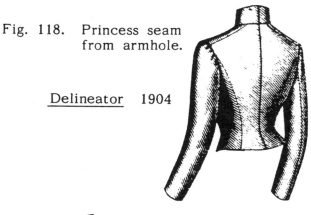

Delineator 1904

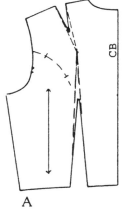

A

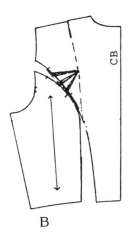

B

Fig. 121.

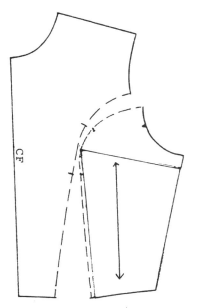

Fig. 119.   Princess seam from armhole.

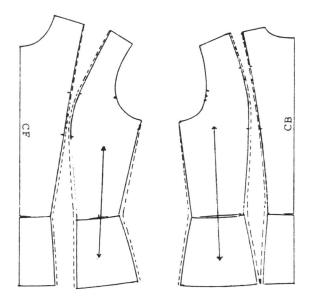

PRINCESS SEAMED BODICE OR JACKET
1.   Cut peplum from top of skirt, and move waist dart to match bodice seam line (Fig. 121).
2.   Draw CF and CB lines on fresh paper. Tape bodice to paper, matching CF and CB lines.   Cut peplum apart and tape to bodice, matching CF, CB and side seams. Add width to peplum as needed.
3.   Smooth curves at waist, and flare hem.
4.   Complete pattern.   New grain line should be centered in side panels, or parallel with CF.

This can be used as a sloper or master pattern for many other designs.

For a princess dress, extend the hem, adding flare to the skirt if you wish.

For a jacket, add a small amount at the seam lines and waist (dotted lines Fig. 121).   If it is to be worn over a blouse, you must also lower the armhole and raise the sleeve (see page 79).

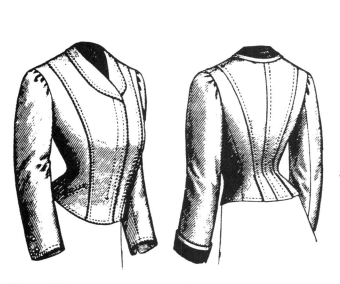

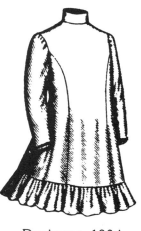

Designer 1904

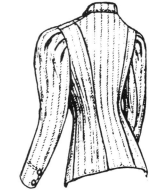

Fig. 120.   McCall's 1908   Delineator 1908

58

SHIRTWAIST

1. Match front and side front of princess sloper at lower bust notch and hem. Tape at bust. If ease was added to the side front at bust dart when you made the sloper, remove it so bust notches match (Fig. 122, a).
2. Slash pattern from below lower notch to corner of shoulder and armhole (b). Spread a small amount through shoulder and bust. Tape to fresh paper. This will add width at the hip line which can be removed from the side seam if necessary. Redraw hem line (c).
3. Extend and lower armhole if you use a shirt sleeve (page 79).

Use the shirtwaist sloper to make a fitted blouse by redrawing the underarm seam to a smooth curve, and making the waist dart more shallow.

For a middy, straighten the underarm seam and omit the waist dart. Use these two variations as slopers for any number of other designs.

Design details can be added by moving darts, adding fullness or cutting yokes.

If the skirt is extended, you have a pattern for a dress with no waistline. Do not add the extra fullness over the bust if you prefer.

Many shirtwaists have a front band like a man's shirt. Sometimes the band folds back upon itself exposing the wrong side of the fabric. At other times it is made as described here.

1. Add paper to CF of bodice front pattern. Draw lines a and b (Fig. 123 A) the width of a narrow band. Draw another line (c) the same distance apart.
2. Decide on the width of the top-stitching (usually 1/8", although in doll size it could be less). Cut pattern apart on line a, and spread 3 times the width of the top-stitching (B). This extension is included but not shown in the remaining diagrams.
3. Fold on fold line b, and again on a, enclosing the raw edge (C). Top-stitch through all layers.
4. Press material (or paper pattern) back against this stitching to form a tuck (D). Stitch again along outer fold. Locate buttonholes vertically on CF.

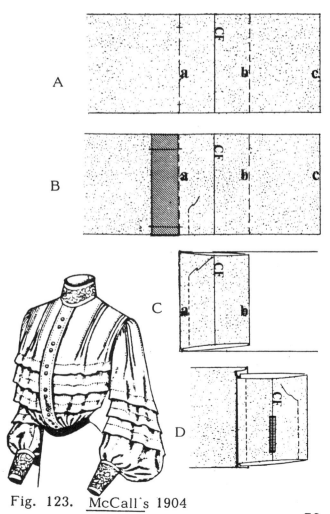

Fig. 123. McCall's 1904

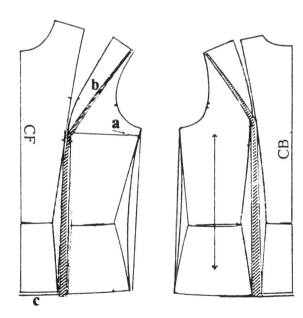

Fig. 122.

Jacket dresses (or basques) in the 1800's very often had straight fronts, sometimes shaped by darts, and princess seamed backs. The side back section was attached to the front, with the underarm seam converted to a dart. Sloping shoulders were· the ideal; so the shoulder seam was moved to the back and slanted from neck to armhole. The armhole seam extended beyond the shoulder point.

Fig. 124 shows a typical pattern from 1880. Note the unfamiliar shape of the armhole, especially at the side back. (The sleeve shape was also different than we are familiar with. See page 80 for a description.)

1. Start with your princess seam sloper. Match at shoulder and tape (Fig. 125 A, a). Likewise, close back shoulder dart. Draw a new shoulder line slanting from neck to armhole. Mark notches across it and cut pattern apart. Tape the cut off shoulder section to bodice front (b).
2. Slash front armhole from shoulder to notch and spread (c). Slash and spread back armhole to correspond (d).

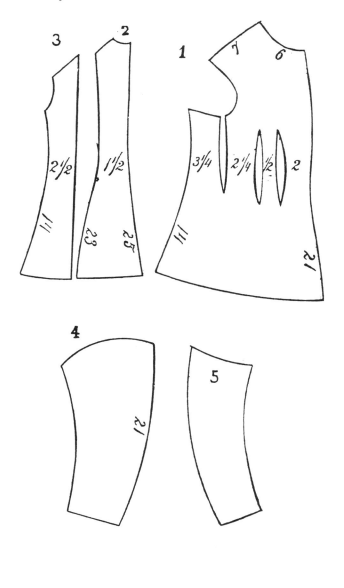

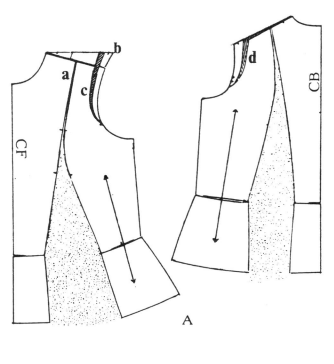

A

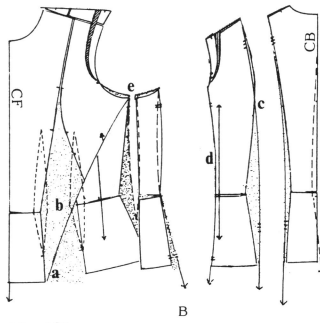

B

Fig. 124. Godey's 1880

Fig. 125.

3. Tape bodice front to fresh paper, filling the space of the waist dart. Notice that the pattern from 1880 has an almost straight front, while your pattern flares toward the hem. To narrow your pattern and remove some of the flare, slash from hem to corner of armhole and side seam. Lap pattern to desired shape (B, a). You have still added some fullness at the hip line.

4. Measure width of dart at the waist, and divide less than this amount into two new darts (b). While the garment has darts in the front, it is not tight fitting at the waist. (Sometimes these darts are not stitched.)

5. Draw a new princess line in the bodice back, making allowance for the shoulder dart (c). The illustration shows a straight line on the side back. Mark notches. (Princess line could also go into armhole.)

6. Draw a slightly curved line from armhole to hem (d). Mark notches. Cut pattern apart. Tape the underarm back section to the bodice front, matching at the armhole level, but leaving a space open (e). Lap peplum to remove some flare. Draw underarm dart. Raise armhole a little.

7. Tape pattern pieces to fresh paper, and redraw seams and CF to conform to the 1880 pattern shapes. These design lines are tentative and must be tested in fabric, and corrected by fitting.

Delineator 1885

Delineator 1885

Harper's Bazar 1881

Delineator 1888

Harper's Bazar 1881

Fig. 126.   Illustrations used by permission

10
Collars

Let your mind run free and make a list of all the neck finishes and collars you can recall. Your list will be long, indeed, if you include everything from simple concealed facings, through lace bindings and frills, to all sorts of collar designs: plastron, Peter Pan, turtle neck, shirt, Mandarin, cape, shawl, Medici and ripple, to name just a few.

If you sincerely want your clothing to have a distinctive, professional look, then learn to design and make a variety of beautiful and suitable neck finishes and collars.

Design quality in costume is judged by how well the garment complements the appearance and personality of the wearer. Becoming clothes accent personality, and coordinate with the color of the complexion, hair and eyes. The neckline is usually the center of interest in clothing because it draws attention to the face. Experiment with many different ways to finish and decorate necklines from simple facings to elaborate collars, and enhance the design quality of the clothes you make.

Necklines are designed in many shapes including round, square, oval, high, low, off-the-shoulder, symmetrical or asymmetrical. They can be finished with facings, bindings or collars. They present you with an opportunity to exercise your imagination to the limit, rewarding your enterprise with distinctive and satisfying costumes.

The necklines and finishes in Figs. 127 and 128 show a few of many possibilities. Some are classic, while others seem quite novel.

The low scalloped neckline (Fig. 127 A) is trimmed with tucks, lace and flowers. In (B), the low scoop is filled with rows of gathered lace. (C), has a net inset with gathered heading, and a lace stole caught with bows at the shoulder.

An Erté design in Fig. 128 is dramatic. It is built up very high, and slashed at the neck edge to admit a scarf. Renée wrapped her dress in a large stole tied on the shoulder. Poiret draped gold tulle above pearl-embroidered gold tissue.

Fig. 127.

Godey's 1880

Reprinted from Harper's Bazar 1895.

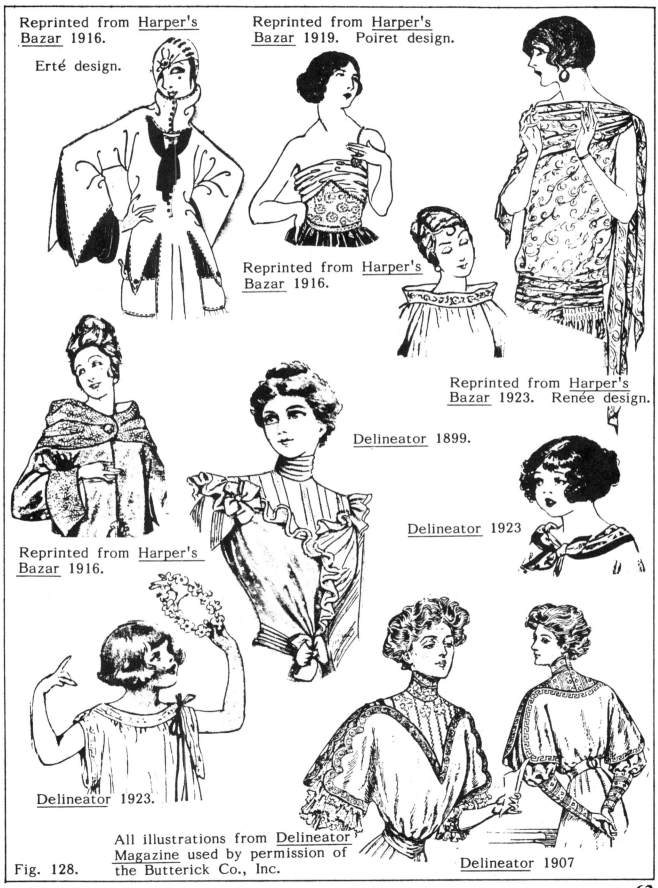

Reprinted from Harper's Bazar 1916.

Erté design.

Reprinted from Harper's Bazar 1919. Poiret design.

Reprinted from Harper's Bazar 1916.

Reprinted from Harper's Bazar 1923. Renée design.

Delineator 1899.

Delineator 1923

Reprinted from Harper's Bazar 1916.

Delineator 1923.

All illustrations from Delineator Magazine used by permission of the Butterick Co., Inc.

Fig. 128.

Delineator 1907

63

Wearing comfort is not a factor in designing necklines and collars for dolls. The choice depends on suitability for the doll, costume and effect desired.

A beautifully designed, constructed and finished collar will enhance a doll's costume. However, small scale clothes frequently need shortcuts to avoid bulk. A collar normally finished at the neck with a facing might simply have the seam allowance removed on the inside, and the cut edge whipped into place. Or the seam allowance can be turned under and sewn invisibly.

A lace or bias binding is probably the simplest finish for a round or oval neckline, whether high or low. For dolls, sew it over the cut edge. Lace can be folded in half and sewn invisibly by hand with tiny stitches and fine thread, catching both lace edges at once. Bias should be stitched with its right side toward the garment, then turned, pressed, folded and overcast into place on the wrong side. Both lace and bias are flexible and conform smoothly to curves when they are not too wide. They have to be mitered at the corners when used on a square neck.

Fig. 129.

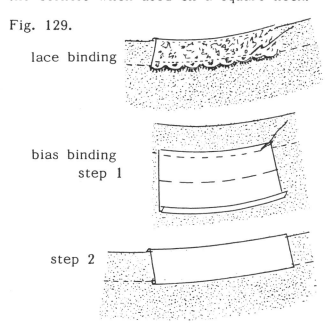

lace binding

bias binding
step 1

step 2

High round necklines can be finished with a frill of lace, or a frill of lace sewn to a stand-up band of lace or ribbon. In the first case, stitch the lace to the right side of the garment and press seam allowance to the inside.

Reprinted from Harper's Bazar 1892.

Fig. 130.

A stand-up band can be stitched to the right side of the neckline with the seam allowance up. If you stay-stitch the neckline first, it makes application easier. A lace frill trims the upper edge of the band. The inside will be neater if the raw edges are completely enclosed by an inner band, but this is not absolutely necessary in dolls' clothes. Or the edge can be finished with wider lace folded in half and applied as a binding. Attach a lace frill to the top edge. Again, stay-titching the neckline first helps.

Also easy and effective is to make a ruffle by gathering a length of lace. If the gathering threads are close to the straight edge (1/8"), then bind the neckline with lace or bias. If you leave a heading (1/4" or more) on a lace ruffle, you can sew it directly to the neckline. Cover gathering threads with narrow lace, ribbon or braid (Fig. 131).

Reprinted from Harper's Bazar 1895.

Reprinted from Harper's Bazar 1893.

Fig. 131.

Delineator 1888

In Fig. 132 the yoke or inset is made from a straight strip of fabric, net or lace gathered with a heading to make a frill at the throat. The neckline of the dress is also gathered with a heading, making an attractive finish.

Fig. 132.

Reprinted from Harper's Bazar 1894.

A single-layer collar can be used when the usual double-layer construction is too bulky. Use only the top collar and stitch it to the wrong side of the neckline, then turn and press, sandwiching seam allowances between dress and collar. This is better in a plain collar than a gathered one, since turning gathers back upon themselves produces bulk.

Another easy and useful method for dolls is to stitch the collar to the right side of the garment, press seam allowance to the inside, and cover raw edges with bias, net or lace (Fig. 133).

The outer edge of a collar can be finished by trimming with lace, turning the seam allowance under and gluing, or covering the stitches with braid.

Reprinted from Harper's Bazar 1891.

Fig. 133.

Lovely handkerchiefs can be used as almost-instant collars. In Fig. 138 A, a square is cut from the center, and gathering threads put around the edge. Cut at center back and hem edges. The one in (B) has a circle cut from the center, with the back opening located in a corner. Experiment with collar patterns developed later in this chapter to see if they can be cut from handkerchiefs.

Be creative and experiment with all sorts of necklines and collars.

Delineator 1895

A

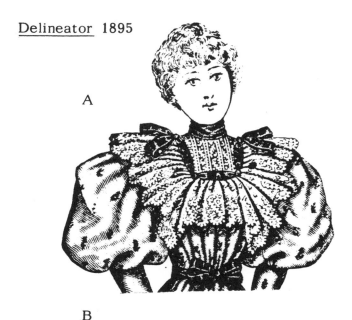

B

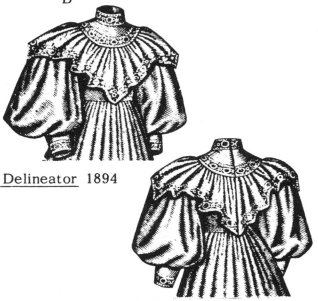

Delineator 1894

Illustrations used by permission of the Butterick Co., Inc.

Fig. 134.

FACINGS
(Review Chap. 7)

A facing is an exact duplicate of the area it faces, used to finish and support the neckline edge. To eliminate bulk, darts or added fullness are folded out of the pattern before the facing is cut. The shoulder seam can be eliminated, but this changes the grain line in one piece. Straight grain can be either at CB or CF.

To make a neckline facing (Fig. 135):
1. Close shoulder dart in bodice back.
2. Match the shoulder seam lines of bodice back and bodice front.
3. Trace CF, CB and neckline. Mark shoulder.
4. Measure width of the facing.
5. Establish grain line.

This facing duplicates the basic high round neckline. If the neckline is a different shape, the facing will duplicate it in the same way, and may or may not have joining seams eliminated.

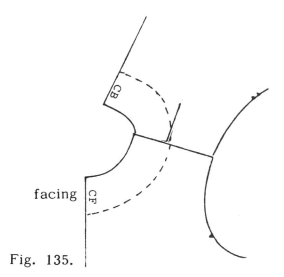

facing

Fig. 135.

COLLARS

When you design a collar, first perfect the neckline. Sometimes the neckline is lowered for comfort, or slightly raised to be more attractive.

Next, develop the roll of the collar; so that it fits against the neck and is as high as your design indicates.

Then, tentatively draw the outer edge. Cut your pattern in cloth and try it on the doll to perfect it and add details.

Note: When you sew a collar, take a slightly deeper seam allowance in the outer and neck edge of the under collar; to keep it from peeking out below the upper collar. You can do this by slipping the upper collar a little inside the edge of the under collar, causing it to bubble slightly at the corners. Measure seam width from edge of the under collar. At the neck, slip the under collar slightly beyond the edge, and sew on the bodice neckline. The fabric thickness governs how much smaller the under collar must be.

Remember the principle of the rings: to fit one ring inside another, the inner one must be smaller. The thickness of the outer ring determines how much smaller the inner one needs to be (Fig. 136).

Fig. 136.

A facing does not make an effective collar. Most collars have some change made in their neckline shape to concave, convex or straight, and some corresponding change in the length of their outer edge. Fig. 137 illustrates how the relationship of the neckline to the outer edge determines the amount of roll or stand of a collar.

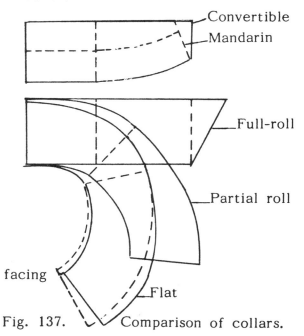

Convertible
Mandarin
Full-roll
Partial roll
facing
Flat

Fig. 137. Comparison of collars.

Collars are classified and described according to their neck edge configuration, degree of roll, and silhouette or outer edge design.

Three terms are used in reference to roll collars. The <u>stand</u> is the height or distance from neck edge to the roll. In a full-roll collar, its width is limited by the length of the neck and the hair line.

The <u>roll</u> or <u>break line</u> is where the collar changes direction. It is usually sharper or more pronounced at the back of the neck; since collars flatten at the front opening, unless they are closed at that point.

The <u>fall</u> is the distance from the roll to the outer edge of the collar. It is longer than the stand; to cover the neckline seam. As the collar becomes flatter, the greater the fall can be in relation to the stand.

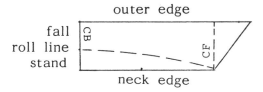

Fig. 138.

PLASTRON COLLAR

A plastron collar is perfectly flat, very much like a facing, and may not be stitched to the garment neckline. If it is to be worn loose, make the neckline slightly smaller; to hide the neck edge of the dress (Fig. 139).

Harper's Bazar 1895

Delineator 1917

Fig. 139.

FLAT COLLAR

A flat collar can be wide or narrow, and its outer edge any shape. It has a slight roll to give it lift, and to cover the neckline seam. To develop roll, lap the bodice front and back patterns at the shoulder in a wedge (Fig. 140).

Close shoulder dart of bodice back. Join shoulder seam lines of bodice front and back; so they just meet at the neckline, but lap at the armhole (a), thus changing the shape of the neckline. (Compare with facing shape.)

Trace CB, neckline and CF. Measure and draw width of the flat collar.

You could also slash the facing pattern at the shoulder and lap the edges to make a similar adjustment.

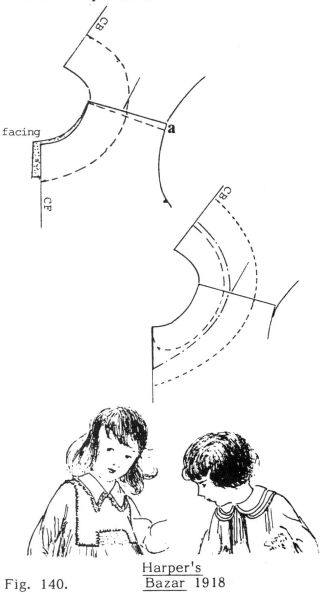

Fig. 140.

Harper's Bazar 1918

Many variations can be made from the basic flat collar. If more roll is desired, then lap more out at the shoulder. Lower the neckline in front or back, then design the collar. When the front and back are separate, draw the collar slightly smaller and stretch it to fit. Outer edge can be designed as you prefer.

Delineator 1921

Fig. 141. Delineator 1920

Sailor collars are made from the flat collar. The outer edge can have many variations (Fig. 142).

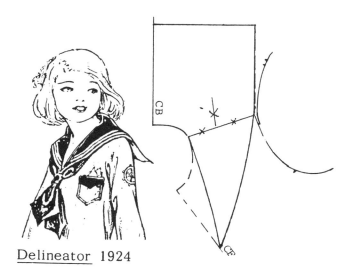

Delineator 1924

All illustrations from Delineator Magazine used by permission of Fig. 142. the Butterick Co., Inc.

PARTIAL-ROLL COLLAR

A partial-roll collar is made by slashing the facing pattern in several places along the outer edge to remove length. The amount of roll determines how much length is removed (Fig. 143).
1. Start with a facing pattern.
2. Slash and lap at outer edge as shown. The more you decrease the length of the outer edge, the more roll will result. Notice that the neck edge curve becomes shallower.
3. The collar will need additional width at the back to compensate for the stand which develops as the roll is increased (a).
4. The designing of the outer edge can be done most effectively in fabric on the figure. Continue to make adjustments in the outer edge until the desired roll is achieved, and the width is adequate for the design.
5. Further design features can then be developed, such as a pointed or rounded front.

Fig. 143.

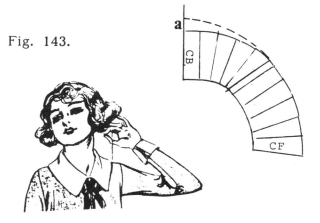

Delineator 1921

Delineator 1923

FULL-ROLL COLLAR

The full-roll collar is a straight band which can easily be drafted by measuring the neck edge of the bodice with a ruler. Mark CF, shoulder and CB. (Fig. 144).

The stand is limited by the length of neck and the hair line. The fall must be slightly longer than the stand to cover the neckline seam.

Draw the front to conform with your design.

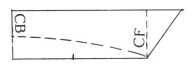

Reprinted from Harper's Bazar 1919.

Delineator 1924

Used by permission of the Butterick Co., Inc.

Fig. 144.   Delineator 1897

Fig. 145.

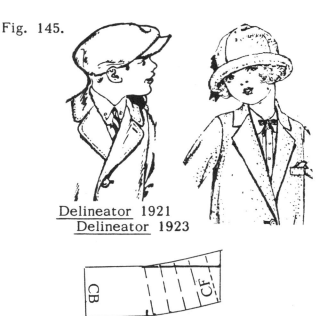

Delineator 1921
Delineator 1923

CONVERTIBLE COLLAR

The convertible collar is a variation of the full-roll collar, and may be worn open at the front. It is slightly convex in the front, causing it to hug the neck. It looks shorter than the full-roll collar, but the neckline measures the same (Fig. 145).

Slash the outer edge of a full-roll collar pattern between CF and shoulder. Lap edges until neck edge curves up a little. Redraw outer edge, reducing the front width. Extend bodice at CF for lapel.

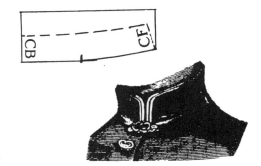

Fig. 146.

MANDARIN COLLAR

The mandarin collar is convex and only half as wide as a roll collar; since it is all stand. It can be made from a convertible collar pattern by tracing the lower half as shown. CF can be straight or curved (Fig. 146).

STRAIGHT-BAND COLLAR

The turtle-neck collar is a straight-band full-roll collar. When made of knitted fabric, it can pull on over the head. It can also open in the back. Raise the neckline a little at CF to make the collar hug the neck (Fig. 147).

A band, either bias or straight grain, can also be used on a lowered neckline. Because it is a straight band attached to curves, it will stand away from the neckline. It can be stitched like a binding, or faced. The ends can be extended to form ties.

A kimono has a straight band attached as a binding.

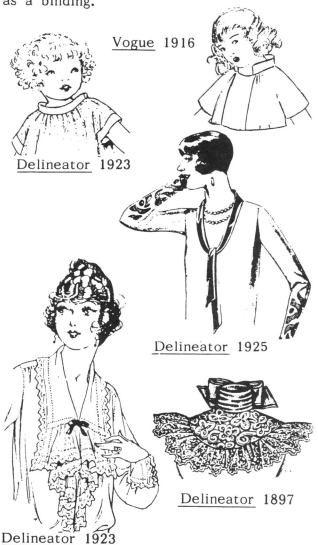

Vogue 1916

Delineator 1923

Delineator 1925

Delineator 1897

Delineator 1923

Fig. 147.

When the neckline is low in front or back the collar will fold in the center and flatten at the ends.

70

Fig. 148.

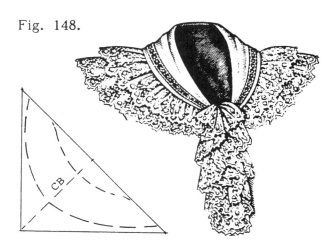

Delineator 1897

FICHU COLLAR

A fichu collar is draped around the neck and often is V-shaped or crossed in the front. It can be made like a scarf tied in the front, with the neck edge on the bias or slightly hollowed out. It can also be made from a straight strip, either bias or straight grain, darted to fit in the back (Fig. 149).

Fig. 149.   Delineator 1899

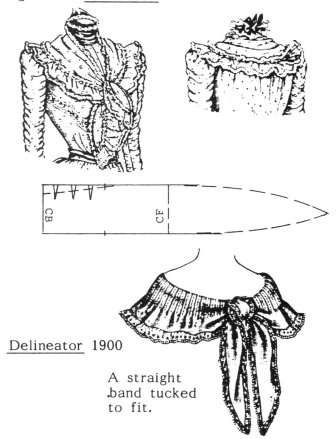

Delineator 1900

A straight band tucked to fit.

CAPE COLLAR

A short cape collar or plastron can be made from the flat collar (Fig. 150 A).

A longer cape is developed by matching the shoulder point of the bodice front and back. Shape the shoulder by a seam or dart. Close the shoulder dart in bodice back, and move to the neck or hem as part of the flare if you wish (B).

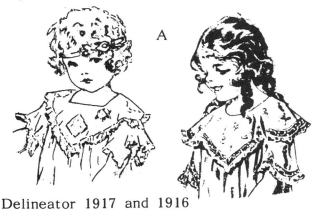

A

Delineator 1917 and 1916

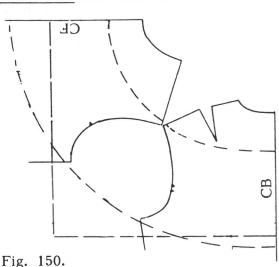

Fig. 150.

B

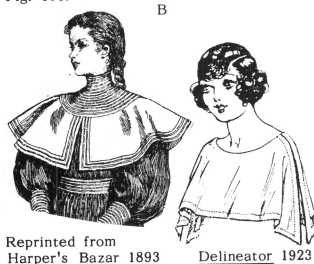

Reprinted from
Harper's Bazar 1893   Delineator 1923

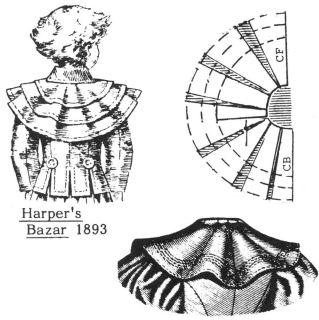

Harper's
Bazar 1893

Fig. 151.   Delineator 1894

RIPPLE COLLAR

The ripple collar has length added to the outside edge (Fig. 151).

1. To add flare, reverse the procedure for making a collar roll, and increase the length of the outer edge by spreading between the slashes. Notice that the neck edge becomes more circular.

2. Remember that slashes must be made where the flare or ripples are to occur. Shape the outer edge as desired.

3. A ripple collar does not have a stand. To make it roll enough to cover the neckline seam, remove a small amount at CB so that the collar must be stretched slightly to fit. Redrawing the neck edge smaller will have the same effect. (Collar B is built up by shaping the seams.)

4. Jabots are made by this method and may be full circles (Fig. 152).

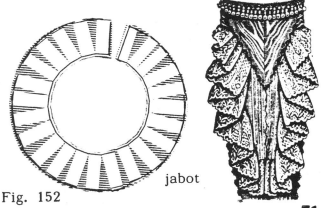

jabot

Fig. 152

FLARED STANDING COLLAR

The Medici or Elizabethan collar stands up from the neckline and is flared at the top. It can be made by darting a straight strip, or by cutting a series of curved seams. It should have the darts or seams boned or otherwise stiffened, or be made of stiff fabric and rely on the darts or seams to hold it up. (Fig. 153.)

BUILT-UP NECKLINE.

A neckline can be built-up or raised by redrawing. Curve the shoulder so that it fits the neck. Collar height is limited by the length of the neck and the hair line.

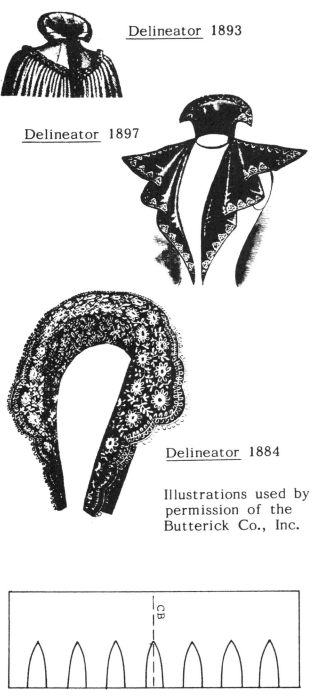

Delineator 1893

Delineator 1897

Delineator 1884

Illustrations used by permission of the Butterick Co., Inc.

Fig. 153.

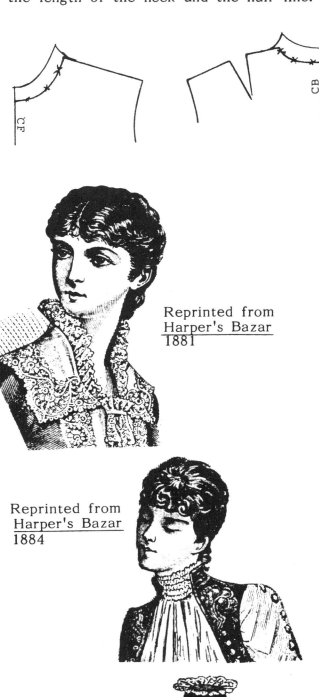

Reprinted from Harper's Bazar 1881

Reprinted from Harper's Bazar 1884

Delineator 1897

Fig. 154.

SHAWL COLLAR

A shawl collar is cut in one with the lapel in the front, and seamed to the back neckline (Fig. 155). It has a CB seam. Move part of the basic dart to CF to provide extra length to outer edge of the collar. Establish roll-line, and design lapel. Extend for collar. Back of collar matches back neckline. Finish with facing.

Fig. 156.

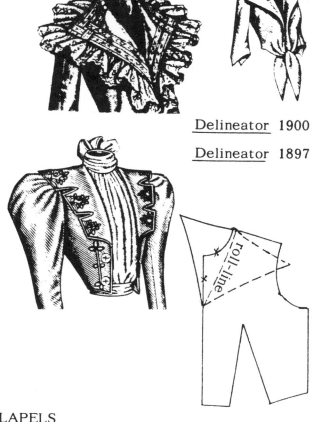

Delineator 1900

Delineator 1897

Fig. 155.

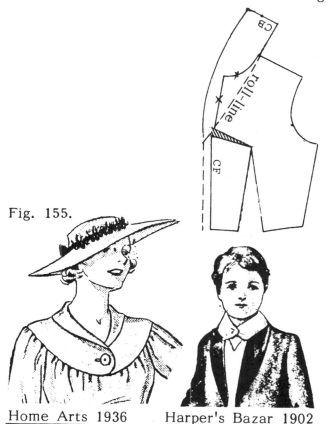

Home Arts 1936   Harper's Bazar 1902

LAPELS

Lapels are a simple extension to the pattern, usually at CF (Fig. 156). Establish the roll-line. Add paper to the pattern, fold on the roll-line and design the lapel.

SUMMARY

A facing is an exact duplicate of the neck edge.

Decreasing length of the outer edge of a collar will result in increased roll.

Increasing the length of the outer edge will result in flare, and decreased roll.

Stretching the neck edge slightly will increase the roll, and easing the collar to the neckline will result in flare.

Develop the stand, roll and set of the collar before designing the outer edge.

Perfect the design in fabric on the figure. Trim such as ruffles, lace or braid is applied after good design lines are developed.

11
Sleeves

Sleeves add interest to clothing, balance the silhouette, and are a conspicuous clue to the date when the costume was in fashion. Further, since dolls' arms sometimes lack good shape or proportion, sleeves can conceal the flaw by puffing out over sagging shoulders, covering the kid leather but revealing lovely bisque hands, or hiding ball joints from view.

To reproduce period fashions, study the fit and proportions of sleeves, as well as style lines.

There are many variations in sleeves, but the two major categories are detached (set-in) or cut-in-one with the bodice (kimono).

SET-IN SLEEVE

SLEEVE TERMS

The cap is the part of the sleeve above the capline. In the basic sleeve, the distance "x" is the arm measurement from shoulder tip to wrist minus the underarm length (Fig. 157).

The capline is a horizontal line between the intersections of cap seam line and underarm seams. It is also the crosswise grain line in the basic sleeve, and the lengthwise grain is perpendicular to it. The shoulder point is slightly to the front of the center line.

The lower curves of the cap seam line are developed from the bodice front and back armholes, and the notches (one in front and two in back) match the bodice front and back. In most designing using the basic set-in sleeve, these curves are not changed, assuring the fit of the under part of the cap seam line to the bodice armhole.

The cap seam line measures slightly longer than the bodice armhole above the notches, and this ease gives the extra fabric needed to fit the top of the sleeve over the upper arm bulge. The larger the arm, the more ease is needed in the cap of the basic sleeve.

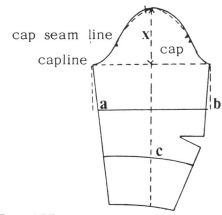

Fig. 157.

Sometimes in fitting, the sleeve cap ease needs to be reduced a small amount. Make the seam line curve more shallow, but do not cut off the top of the sleeve and shorten the cap height.

The elbow dart creates a bulge for the elbow. The hem of a long fitted sleeve is curved to conform to the wrist line.

The basic sleeve can be made into a short sleeve by drawing a straight line above the elbow parallel with the capline. Since the sleeve is fitted, the hemline does not intersect the underarm seam at a right angle and a point develops (Fig. 158 A). This can be corrected by redrawing the underarm seams perpendicular to the capline and new hem (Fig. 157, b).

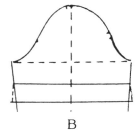

Fig. 158.

If you do not object to the sleeve being slightly shorter at the underarm seam, a folded hem can be used on a short fitted sleeve, but the hem allowance must be widened to conform to the shape of the sleeve. Fold up the hem and cut along the seam lines for the proper shape. Add paper to the pattern if necessary (Fig. 158 B).

To shorten a fitted basic sleeve below the elbow, measure up an even distance from the hem. A curved hem will need a matching facing (Fig. 157, c).

The same principles you learned to use earlier apply in designing sleeves. Lengthy explanations are not given here, except where the applications introduce a new use. Complete the patterns the same as before, with seam allowance, grain line, hem and labels. Test in muslin.

ELBOW DART MOVED TO CAP
1. Extend dart to center of sleeve and close (Fig. 159, a).
2. Slash from cap to dart point as shown.
3. Spread pattern and tape to fresh paper.
4. Redraw capline, adding length if you want it to puff (b).
5. Control fullness with tucks, pleats, gathers, shirring or smocking.
6. Redraw grain line (dotted line c).

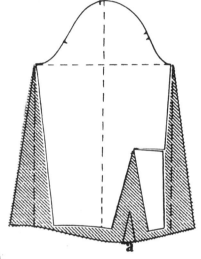

Fig. 160.

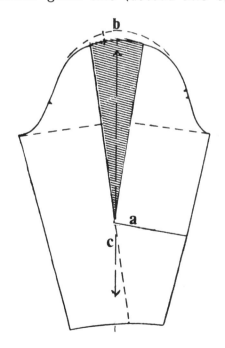

Fig. 159.

ELBOW DART MOVED TO HEM
1. Close dart (Fig. 160).
2. Slash from hem directly below point of dart (at the line of the little finger) to dart.
3. Spread pattern and tape to fresh paper.
4. Straighten side seams, either perpendicular to cap line, or slightly flared. Be sure the seams match in both length and flare.
5. Redraw hem line, adding length for puff.
6. A vent can be constructed (a), but in doll sizes this may be difficult. The opening can be at the underarm seam for dolls, if the design of the cuff will permit it. If a cuff is needed, design and cut it off before the dart is moved.
7. Slash and spread the sleeve if more fullness is desired.

ADDING FULLNESS

Fullness can be added to a sleeve evenly or in a wedge, using the principles you have already learned. Redraw curve and add length when you want it to puff out (Fig. 161).

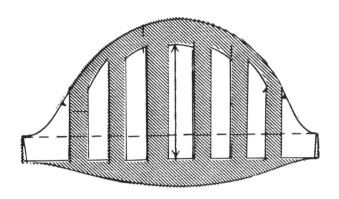

A. short puffed

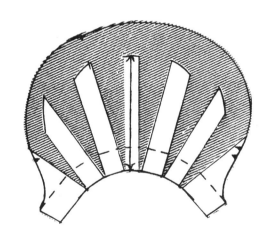

B. puffed at the top

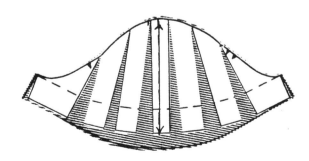

C. flared at the bottom

Fig. 161.

CUFFS

Cuffs complete sleeves, hold hem fullness and contribute to the design of both sleeve and costume. They are usually harmonious with, but subordinate to the collar.

If the cuff will be a straight band, cut off its width from the hem of the sleeve before further work is done. This maintains the correct sleeve length. A straight cuff can be drafted from the hem measurement.

SLEEVE WITH CUFF

1. Draw line for below-elbow length cuff and mark notches.
2. Cut off cuff and add extensions for placket (Fig. 162, a).
3. Close dart.
4. Slash and spread sleeve, moving dart and adding fullness, either evenly or in a wedge.
5. Redraw lower edge and cap, adding length if puff is desired.

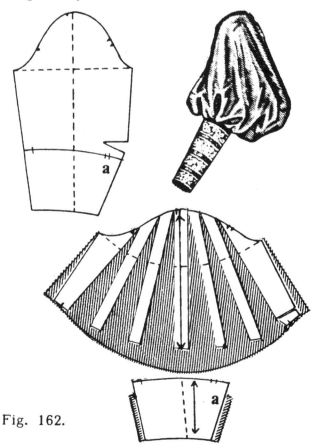

Fig. 162.

A cuff that comes above the elbow must retain the elbow dart. Continue as above.

If you want cuff to open at the placket line or little finger location, then slash across the cuff to the dart point before you cut cuff from sleeve. Tape the cuff together at the underarm seam and add extensions for lap (Fig. 163).

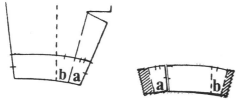

Fig. 163.

A straight cuff can be drafted using the hem measurement. Draw a straight rectangle the desired length and width, adding an extension for the lap (Fig. 164).

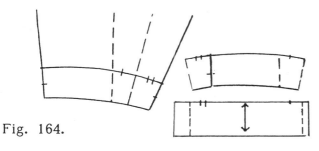

Fig. 164.

SHAPED CUFF

Many kinds of shaped cuffs are used with sleeves. Some are classic while others are quite innovative.

Sketch the design line for the shaped cuff on the basic sleeve. Plan for the opening to come at the placket, or little finger line. Mark notches. If the cuff is separate and joined to the sleeve at the hem, make it slightly larger; so that it lies smoothly over the sleeve.
1. Draw placket line from hem to dart point at location of little finger (Fig. 165, a).
2. Sketch shape of cuff, having it match in width at the underarm seams (b). Mark notches.
3. Cut through cuff from hem to dart point. Close elbow dart.
4. Make copy of cuff. Tape together at underarm seam. Draw extension for the lap. A cuff should be lined for a neat finish.
5. Slash and spread sleeve. Make a placket above cuff.

If the cuff is stitched to the sleeve, it is developed the same as a yoke.

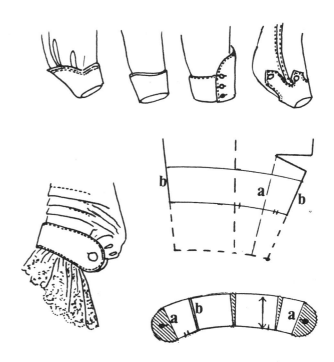

Fig. 165.

FRILL

A frill can be flared, or a straight grain ruffle.
1. Draw the cuff, and mark notches (a).
2. Draw the shaped frill. The longest point will come at the little finger (b).
3. Cut pattern apart. Slash and spread frill. It may be spread to be a full circle.
4. Slash and spread upper sleeve to add fullness and puff.

Delineator 1904

band

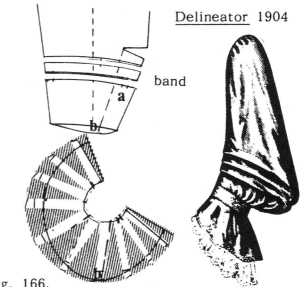

Fig. 166.

DESIGNING IN A DART

Many dramatic sleeves have design features in the elbow dart space (Fig. 168).
If the design comes at the little finger:
1. Draw in the placket line and slash the sleeve from that location to the cap.
2. Close elbow dart and redraw back underarm seam if necessary.
3. Spread sleeve the desired amount. Lap slightly at the cap for a smoother line if you wish.
4. Design in the space according to your illustration.

If you want to move fullness toward center, extend elbow dart and continue.

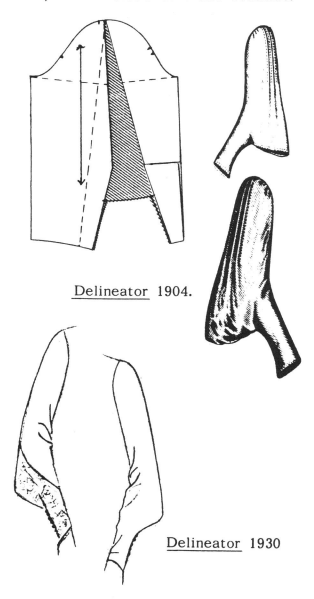

Delineator 1904.

Delineator 1930

Fig. 167.

Fig. 168.

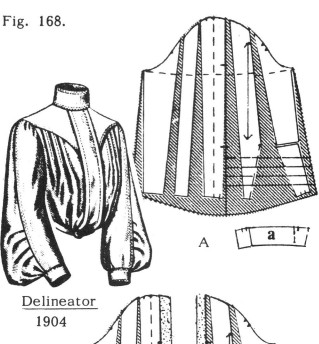

A   a

Delineator
1904

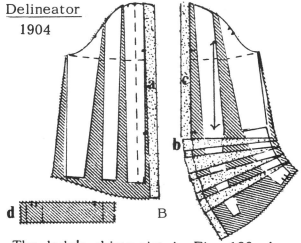

d   B

The lady's shirtwaist in Fig. 168 has a novel two-piece sleeve with added fullness.
1. Measure and draw cuff line. Mark notches.
2. Slash at placket line. Cut off cuff and tape underarm seams together (A, a).
3. Move dart. Slash and spread pattern, adding small amount of fullness at the cap, and flaring the hem. Straighten underarm seams. Draw new cap seam line and vertical grain line. Redraw cap and hem.
4. Draw line for vertical seam. Mark notches. Cut sleeve apart and add facing extension to sleeve front (B, a).
5. Draw lines for tucks in sleeve back as shown in illustration. Slash and spread (b).
6. Add extension for underlap (c). Draw length of tucks and fold closed to cut edge of sleeve.
7. Draft cuff from measurements of cut-off section, add extension for lap (d).

SHIRT SLEEVE

This sleeve is popular because it is comfortable to wear and easy to sew. Understanding how it is developed will help explain some of the unfamiliar sleeve shapes seen in period patterns. Many period sleeves had shallow caps with little or no curve under the arm, and the shape of the armhole varied from quite shallow to deeply curved. When the shape of the sleeve and armhole are dissimilar, the sleeve will not set smoothly in the armhole. In some cases the sleeve was eased to fit under the arm, as well as over the cap.

The crosswise grain line of a shallow-cap sleeve will not be horizontal, as in the basic set-in sleeve, but will slant upward. In a short sleeve, a straight grain hem will be lifted. In a long, cuffed sleeve, additional length must be provided, or the sleeve will pull and be uncomfortable to wear.

The relationship of the shape of the armhole of the bodice and the curve of the underarm and cap of the sleeve determines how the sleeve will fit.

1. Lower the armhole on the bodice front and back (Fig. 169 A and C); the amount depends upon the size of the pattern you are using. In a full size human pattern, lower the armhole 1".
2. Raise the underarm curve of the sleeve the same amount (B, a). The arm hole of the bodice has been lowered. In order for the sleeve to be comfortable to wear and not pull, additional length must be added to the underarm. Add width to underarm seam (b).
3. Widen shoulder of bodice front and back armhole by slashing and spreading the same amount. Redraw shoulder. Shirts usually have extended shoulders. When they do not, this step can be omitted. Remove the amount you added to the shoulder from the sleeve cap (c).
4. Measure the bodice armhole and compare with sleeve measurement. Re-draw cap of sleeve to conform to this measurement, plus a small amount of ease (d).
5. Move elbow dart of sleeve to hem, and straighten underarm seams (D). Re-draw lower edge to compensate for lowered cap and also for puff. (If a cuff is used, cut it off before moving elbow dart, B.)
6. Complete the pattern; add seam allowance and hems where needed.
7. Cut pattern in muslin and try on to check fit. Notice that the crosswise grain line of the sleeve is no longer horizontal. Fitting folds will develop under the arm, and these vertical folds are characteristic of shirt sleeves.

NOTE: You can also start with your shirtwaist sloper.

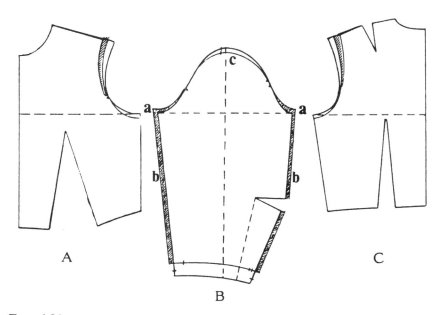

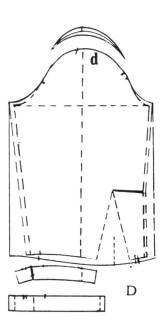

Fig. 169.

TWO-PIECE SLEEVE

A sleeve with two seams follows the curve of the arm; fitting somewhat better than the basic sleeve. It is harder to sew into the armhole in dolls' clothes unless the back seam coincides with a princess seam to the armhole. Two-piece sleeves were once used extensively. but now they are found primarily in men's suits.

1. Extend elbow dart to front seam and tape closed.
2. Fold side seams so that they meet at the center. Tape together at underarm and hem (Fig. 170 A). They may bulge between these points.
3. Draw new seam lines about 1/3 of the distance from folds to seam on the underside of the sleeve. Mark notches. (Some period sleeves had much narrower under sleeves; make pattern conform to your design.)
4. Cut sleeve apart on new seam lines (B). Open elbow darts in both upper and under sleeves. Draw grain line.
5. Tape upper and under sleeves to fresh paper and redraw new seam lines to gentle curves.

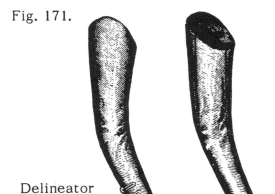

Fig. 171.

Delineator
1885

1880s SLEEVE

For jacket developed on page 60.

1. Raise underarm of two-piece sleeve to match raised armhole in bodice (Fig. 172).
2. Slash under sleeve from underarm to hem. and to intersection of side seams and underarm. Raise underarm seam and spread sleeve to match. (Sleeve must fit armhole, and redrawing without adding width would make it too small.)
3. Measure and remove the same amount from the sleeve cap as you added to the jacket shoulder (a).
4. Slash upper sleeve from cap to hem. and to intersections of cap and side seams. Lower cap and spread sleeve.

This sleeve will not fit the same as a basic sleeve because the cap height is shortened; in fact, it fits more like a tight shirt sleeve. Slashing and spreading horizontally at the elbow will add some length to the sleeve (b), resulting in the more pronounced curve seen in period patterns. Also, because the sleeve is raised under the arm. joining it to the armhole will push it down, causing characteristic wrinkles.

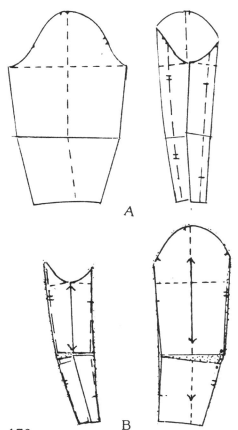

A

B

Fig. 170.

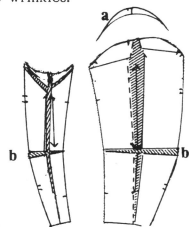

a

b   b

Fig. 172.

LEG O' MUTTON

The Leg O' Mutton sleeve was a popular design in the late 1880s when sleeves became greatly exaggerated. Caps reached their maximum width in the mid 1890s.

Intricate pattern and dressmaking skills were required to achieve the desired effects. The large sleeves needed to be lined or underlined with crinoline to keep them from drooping. In addition, they were often supported by "plumpers", "sleeve bustles" or whalebone hoops. Net or tissue can be stuffed in dolls' sleeves to hold them out.

There are several ways to develop a pattern for a Leg O' Mutton sleeve. All involve slashing and spreading the basic pattern to add fullness to the sleeve cap. Leave the elbow dart or move it to the cap as you choose.
1. Close elbow dart.
2. Slash basic sleeve pattern from the cap seam line to the point where you want the fullness to begin (Fig. 173 A, a).
3. Slash from this cut to the side seams in two or three places (b). Spread the pattern (B). Be sure the curves of front and back underarm seams match (a).
4. Redraw the cap adding length for the puff (b).
5. Redraw grain line (c) and mark shoulder point (d). (The sleeve could also be cut on the bias.)
6. Extend the underarm seam for a placket at the wrist (e). The hem can be finished with a facing, bias band or lace frill.

Fig. 174.

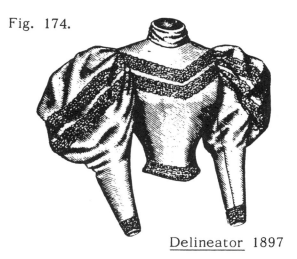

Delineator 1897

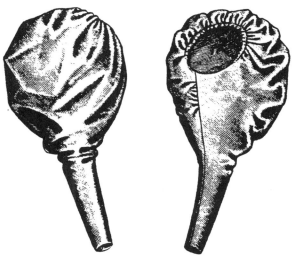

Delineator 1893

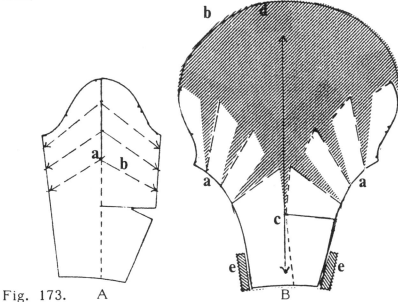

Fig. 173.   A   B

Delineator 1894

81

TWO PIECE LEG O' MUTTON SLEEVE
Develop fullness in upper sleeve the same as for a one-piece sleeve.

If additional width is wanted, slash and spread pattern at underarm. Gather or tuck to fit (Fig. 175).

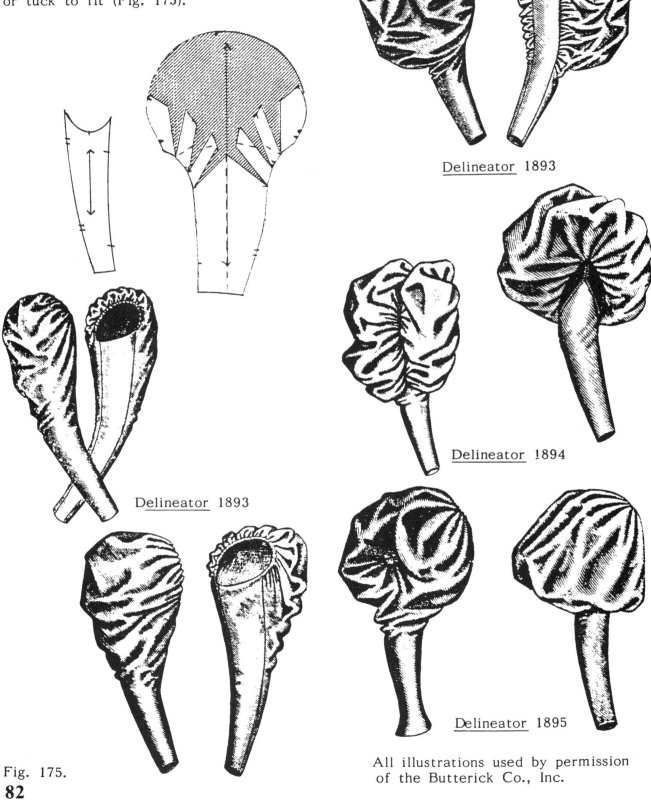

Fig. 176.

Delineator 1893

Delineator 1893

Delineator 1894

Delineator 1895

Fig. 175.

All illustrations used by permission of the Butterick Co., Inc.

SLEEVE CUT IN BODICE

There are many types of sleeves cut-in-one with the bodice, ranging from simple caps on sleeveless bodices, to kimono, dolman or raglan styles. Sometimes these sleeves are joined to the bodice by purely decorative seams. In large sizes, fabric width may require the pattern to be divided into smaller parts. The kimono sleeve pattern can be used as a sloper for making other designs.

Fig. 177. <u>Delineator 1921</u>

KIMONO SLEEVE

1. Prepare sleeve (Fig. 178).
   a. Fold the basic sleeve in half at the cap and hem and mark these two points.
   b. Measure a small distance (1/2" in human size) toward the front and mark at cap and hem.
   c. Join these points with a straight line (a). Measure down from the cap a small amount (again, 1/2" in human size), and mark (b).
   d. Cut pattern apart.

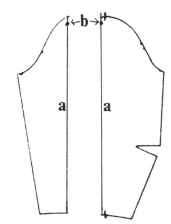

Fig. 178.

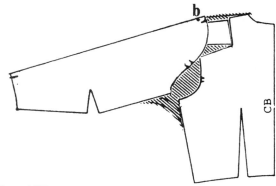

Fig. 179.

2. Prepare bodice back (Fig. 179).
   a. Move shoulder dart to armhole, above the notches. Raise shoulder.
   b. Join sleeve cap at (b) to raised shoulder. Pivot underarm to lap slightly, or leave a gap depending on how much fullness you want under the arm. Tape into place. (If the sleeve laps over the bodice, then you must design a gusset to replace the lost ease.) Redraw the underarm as a curve. The higher the curve, the closer the fit.

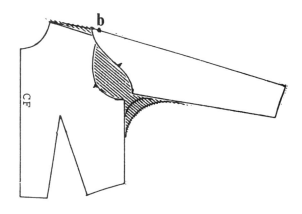

Fig. 180.

3. Prepare bodice front (Fig. 180).
   a. Raise shoulder the same amount as bodice back.
   b. Join sleeve cap to raised shoulder at (b), and to underarm the same as you did on bodice back. Tape.
   c. Move underarm dart to waist or shoulder according to your design.
   d. Redraw underarm curve to match back.
4. Test in muslin and make corrections as necessary.

Your kimono sloper can be used to make other designs. If you join the bodice front and back along the sleeves (Fig. 181 A), the entire bodice can be cut in one piece, with a dart at the shoulder. Notice that either front or back could be cut on straight grain, but not both. The sleeve could be cut on any design line (three are shown). Line (c) follows the curve of the hem. The sleeve could be cut in one piece and the bodice front and back cut with their centers on straight grain. The sleeve could also be shortened, or have a design feature added.

If the shoulder seams are joined (B), flare develops at the hem of the sleeve. This could be gathered, tucked or pleated.

The underarm seam can be redrawn to a lower curve as shown by the dotted lines.

Fig. 182.

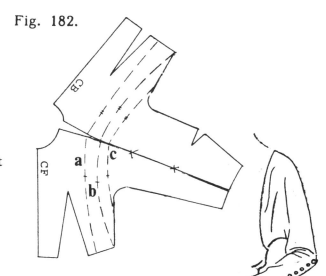

SIMPLIFIED DOLMAN

To make simplified dolman sleeves the bodice and sleeve can be cut apart vertically. Three possibilities are shown (Fig. 182 a, b, and c). The bodice front and back would be cut separately with their centers on straight grain, and the sleeve cut in one piece.

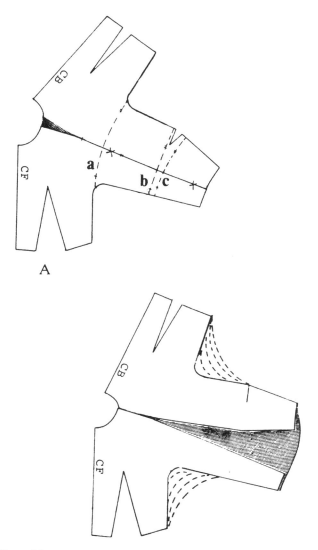

A

Fig. 181.   B

Fig. 183.

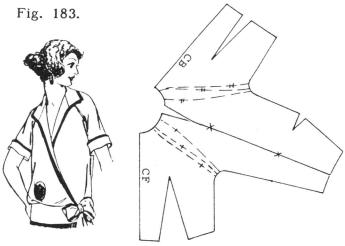

LOOSE RAGLAN

The simplest way to make a raglan sleeve is to draw transitional lines from neckline to underarm seam on your kimono sloper (Fig. 183). Three possibilities are shown. Mark notches and cut pattern apart on the design lines. Other designing can be done in the sleeve and by moving the shoulder dart.

FITTED RAGLAN

1. Lower armhole of bodice front and back (Fig. 184 A, a). Draw underarm seams slightly wider if you want more ease. Draw a transitional line from neck to below armhole notches (b). This should not be a straight line, but follow the curve near the underarm and the shoulder at the top. Mark notches.
2. Tape sleeve to fresh sheet of paper and extend grain line at the shoulder point (B). Raise the sleeve the same amount as you lowered the bodice armhole (c), and widen the sleeve to match bodice (d).
3. Cut off shoulder sections from bodice front and back and position them on sleeve, matching the armhole notches. If they do not fit easily, slash on the dashed lines in the direction of the arrows, to but not through you design line. Spread so that pattern will match at the top of the sleeve and at the armhole notches. It may lap a little at the cap seam line. Tape into place. Notice that the shoulder seams of the bodice front and back form a large dart.
4. Redraw smoother curves at front and back design lines if angles have developed.

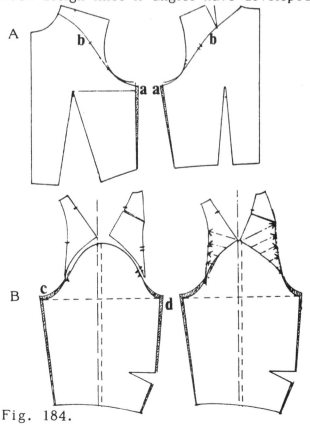

Fig. 184.

Fig. 185.

Delineator 1904

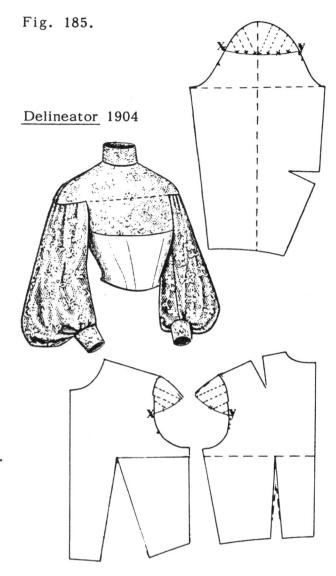

DROPPED SHOULDER

A yoke can be cut from the sleeve cap and joined to the bodice armhole. If it is too long, it restricts arm movement and is likely to tear out. It can be combined with a bodice front and back yoke in a continuous line (Fig. 185).

1. Draw design line for yoke in sleeve cap. Mark notches, and mark location where cap will join bodice front and back armhole.
2. Cut sleeve on design line, and again on lengthwise grain at shoulder mark.
3. Slash from cap seam line to, but not through, the design line (dotted lines). Lap to fit and tape to bodice front and back armholes.
4. Redraw shoulder seam line to a smooth curve.

All illustrations from <u>Delineator</u>
<u>Magazine</u> 1923. Used by
permission of the Butterick Co., Inc.

Fig. 186.

12
Skirts

Skirts give balance and style to dress designs, and with sleeves, are an important part of the garment's silhouette. Their hem length fluctuates with the date, the age of the wearer, and the use of the costume, demanding careful study to determine the most appropriate length for each situation.

Dolls look best in skirts with exaggerated fullness. Two or three times as much fullness can be used for a doll as for a human; since wearing comfort is not a factor.

A tastefully designed and executed skirt gives distinction to a garment, and a correctly developed skirt pattern is necessary to recreate a period costume. With so many design possibilities to choose from, there is no need for trite repetition of plain gathered skirts.

Fullness and design details can be added to skirts in many ways using the pattern making techniques already described.

Design fullness can be added at the top or the bottom.

Flare is fullness added in a wedge.

Pleats, tucks and gathers are made by even-width additions to the basic pattern. These skirts can also be drafted. Measure a straight strip the correct length plus hem, by the desired width.

Yokes are designed and cut into various portions of the pattern.

Extensions and closings can be decorative as well as functional.

All kinds of pockets, tabs, slits, overskirts and drapery enhance skirt styles.

In every skirt design, start with a perfectly fitted pattern. Make the design changes, then complete the pattern with grain lines, seam allowance, hems and facings as needed. Test the pattern in muslin to correct the fit and perfect design lines.

Skirts can be classified in many ways, for pattern making purposes they can be described as fitted, flared or gored, and pleated.

FITTED SKIRTS

Darts and curved side seams mold the fitted skirt above the hip line, and the hem measurement is not much more than that of the hip, thus it has little flare.

A basic skirt pattern is fitted at the waist by darts and the side seam curve (Fig. 187). The hem is slightly flared. CF and CB are cut on straight grain folds.

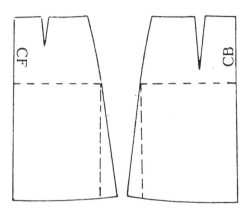

Fig. 187. A fitted skirt.

GORED SKIRTS

As fullness and flare are added, the grain may be changed to give various effects. The lengthwise grain of fabric is usually the strongest, and therefore stretches less than the crosswise grain. True bias is the most unstable. A seam may have any degree of bias between straight grain and true bias.

Bias clings to the figure in soft fabrics and stands away in stiff ones. Because it is unstable, it stretches or sags easily. Carefully consider the effect you want when you decide how you will place the grain on the pattern pieces.

When bias fabric clings, it can be soft and slenderizing. In stripes or plaids interesting chevrons or herringbone designs emerge when bias seams are joined.

The choices for straight grain placement in a 4-gore skirt are shown in Fig. 188. In A, CF (and CB) are cut on straight grain, making the side seam somewhat bias. If more flare is added, the side seam bias increases (dotted lines).

In B, the side seams are cut on straight grain, making CF and CB bias. Straight lines at the hips are slenderizing, and the bias CF and CB are graceful. When cut in striped fabric, an upward or downward pointing chevron will result. If less bias is wanted, small darts, or small darts converted to ease, will make the skirt seams straighter.

In C, straight grain is centered in each panel, making all the seams slightly bias.

Balanced flare is achieved by adding equal amounts to each side seam. This is necessary if you want to match plaids or stripes. The skirt in Fig. 189, shows planned unbalanced flare in a striped skirt.

Reprinted from Harper's Bazar 1916

Fig. 189.

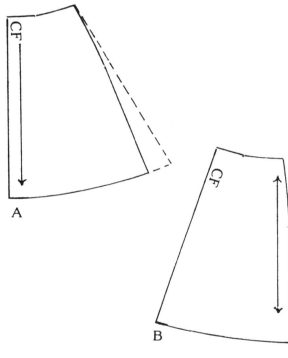

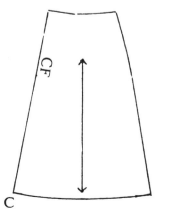

Fig. 188.

88

If more flare is added to one edge than its adjoining seam line, the wider side will fold over the other. If used deliberately, this technique will give interesting effects.

SIDE SEAM ELIMINATED

The side seam can be eliminated in a basic skirt by joining the front and back pattern pieces at the hip line (Fig. 190). A dart forms above the hip line, and the skirt laps below it. If CF and CB are on straight grain, the result is a perfectly straight skirt. The darts can be stitched or converted to tucks or gathers (A). If you want more flare, pivot the skirt at the hip line, making the side hip dart smaller, and shifting flare to the hem (B). If CF is cut on a straight grain fold, then CB is bias. If straight grain is located along the side seam, both CF and CB must be seams.

Fig. 190. Eliminating the side seam.

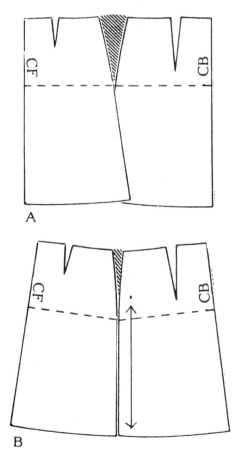

A

B

TWO-GORE SKIRT

Gored skirts can be classified according to the number of gores they have. The basic skirt pattern is a two-gore skirt.

FOUR-GORE SKIRT

1. Add flare at CF and CB (Fig. 191). Straighten curve at side by shifting a similar amount from center seam (A).
2. Convert dart to flare by moving it to the hem (B). Flare can be added at center and/or side seams, (dotted lines).
3. Make additional slashes to distribute increased flare evenly throughout skirt. As more flare is added, remove the hip curve at the side seam (C). Draw new grain lines in all three styles.

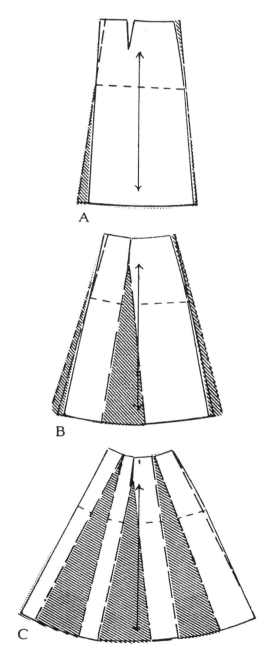

A

B

C

Fig. 191. Four gore skirt.

SIX-GORE SKIRT

The six-gore skirt has one front and two side panels in both front and back. The panels, which are usually flared at the bottom, are attractive and slimming. This style, and its variations, is often found in period designs.

1. Design a pleasing panel for CF and CB and mark notches. (Fig. 192). If the skirt is fitted, bisect the dart, incorporating it into the seam line. Move dart to correspond with the design line.
2. Cut the pattern apart and add flare to each panel by redrawing, or slashing and pivoting (B).
3. Locate straight grain in the side panels either perpendicular to the hip line (a), or centered (b).

SEVEN-GORE SKIRT

The seven-gore skirt is actually a six-gore skirt with a CB seam. The back panels can have fullness added (Fig. 193).

In the late 1880s these panels were cut from full widths of the material and gathered tightly to fit at the waist. This meant that straight grain edges were stitched to bias or flared ones (Fig. 194).

The layout shows the pattern cut from single layer, 24" wide, reversible fabric. Note that the notches are not correct.

Diagram of the skirt.

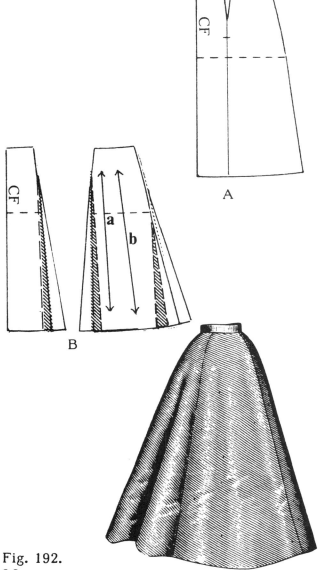

Fig. 192.

Fig. 193.   <u>Ladies' Home Journal</u> 1904

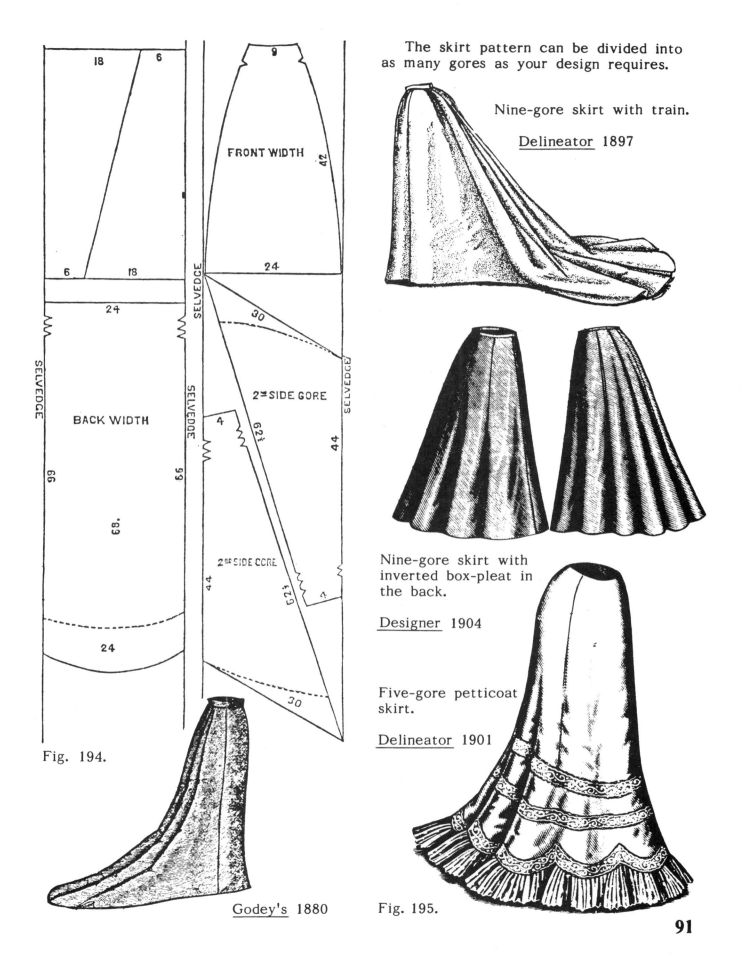

18   6

9

FRONT WIDTH   42

6   18

24

SELVEDGE

24   30

SELVEDGE

2ᴺᴰ SIDE GORE

4   62½   44

BACK WIDTH

SELVEDGE   SELVEDGE

66   66

68.   44   2ᴺᴰ SIDE GORE

62½   4

24   30

Fig. 194.

The skirt pattern can be divided into as many gores as your design requires.

Nine-gore skirt with train.

<u>Delineator</u> 1897

Nine-gore skirt with inverted box-pleat in the back.

<u>Designer</u> 1904

Five-gore petticoat skirt.

<u>Delineator</u> 1901

<u>Godey's</u> 1880

Fig. 195.

91

TRUMPET SKIRT

Graceful trumpet skirts are fitted above the hip line and flare is introduced at the thigh, knee or below (Fig. 196). It is best done at each seam of a multiple-gore skirt, so that the fullness is distributed smoothly. Slash the skirt at a seam line from hem to the point where you want the flare to begin, then spread the desired amount. Flare can be added equally to all the seams, or increased gradually from front to back.

Fig. 196.

Fig. 197.

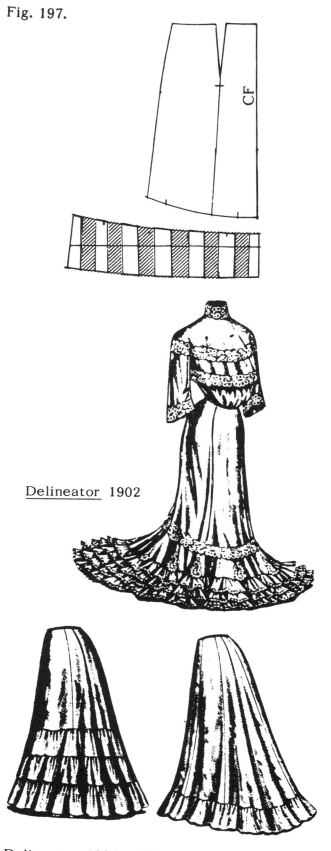

Delineator 1903

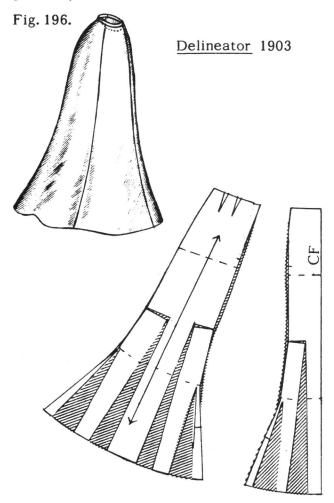

Delineator 1902

FLOUNCES

One or more flounces can be cut into a skirt pattern using the same pattern making techniques you learned earlier. They should all be designed with careful attention to their lines, proportion and scale (Fig. 197).

Even-width flounces can be drafted. If they are in tiers, graduated widths with the smallest at the top are usually the most pleasing.

Delineator 1904. Illustrations used by permission of the Butterick Co., Inc.

92

FLARED SIDE PANEL

1. Lengthen the hem of the basic skirt pattern. Design and cut off front and back panels, adding flare to make them more flattering (Fig. 198 A).
2. Join side front and back, eliminating the side seam.
3. Close all darts and convert to flare (B). Slash and spread pattern.
4. Plan for true bias at the side seam location (a). The amount of flare needed will depend on the cloth. This design should be made in a soft fabric such as crepe or chiffon, and in such a fabric much of the fullness will drape out. Plan also for a nearly straight grain at the front and back seams to match the grain of the front and back panel seams (b).

For dolls, two pretty handkerchiefs could be used for the side panels.

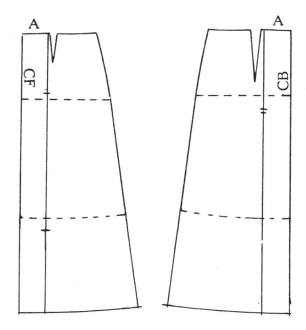

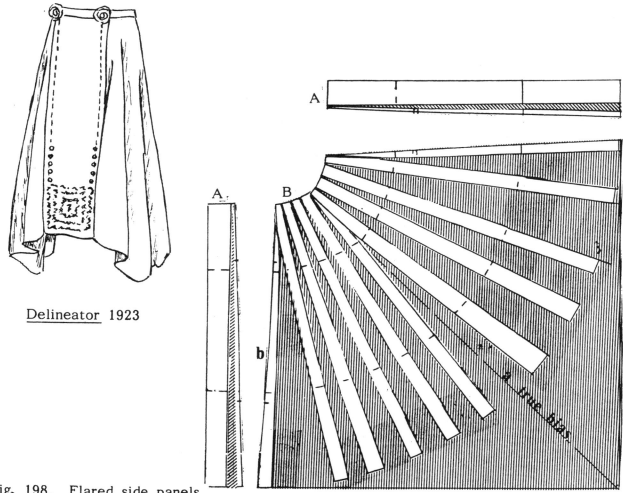

Delineator 1923

Fig. 198. Flared side panels.

YOKES

A yoke is cut in a skirt in the same way as in a bodice or sleeve. Its usual purpose is to provide a fitted hip section with adjoining fullness either flared, pleated, tucked or gathered. It can also be purely decorative.

1. Begin with a perfectly fitted basic skirt pattern. With the skirt on the body, lightly draw the shape of the yoke. The bodice is usually designed first, and it would be wise to have it on the body also, so that the lines of the skirt yoke will be harmonious with it.

2. Correct the lines of the yoke at the table, using a French curve or ruler (Fig. 199). Mark notches.

3. Extend the dart and close (a). Your pattern making will be simplified if the yoke line intersects the point of the dart. Cut the pattern apart.

4. Slash and spread the lower section to add desired fullness. Tape to fresh paper. Complete the pattern.

YOKE WITH A PANEL

This design has flare in the lower section. Additional flare is added near the bottom (Fig. 200). For balanced flare each side is increased the same amount (a). Adding more flare to one edge than its adjoining seam will cause the long side to fold over the short one (b).

Fig. 199. Skirt yokes.

Ladies' Home Journal 1911

Delineator 1904

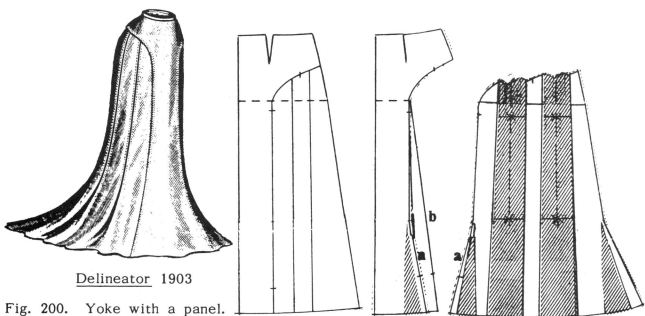

Delineator 1903

Fig. 200. Yoke with a panel.

94

OVERSKIRTS

Overskirts are second skirts that are slashed, draped up or shorter than the underskirt so that parts of it are revealed. The two skirts can be stitched together to the waistline or waist band as a single unit.

Delineator 1907

Delineator 1894

Fig. 201.

PEPLUMS

Peplums are similar to short skirts (usually above hip length) stitched to the waistline of a bodice, or to a waistband, and worn over a skirt (Fig. 202).

Design the peplum in the basic skirt pattern. Cut pattern apart and discard the lower part. Add fullness or flare as your design requires. You must add at least enough so that the peplum will fit smoothly over the skirt.

Fig. 202.

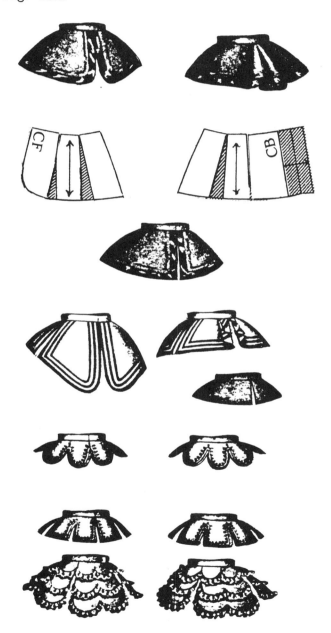

Delineator 1897

MOVING THE WAISTLINE

To lower the waistline, cut a yoke in the top of the skirt pattern and add it to the bodice (Fig. 203).

Fig. 203.

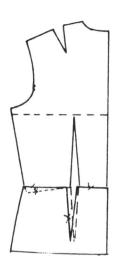

To raise the waistline, cut off a section from the hem of the bodice and add it to the skirt pattern (Fig. 204).

Fig. 204.

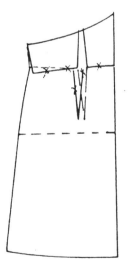

PLEATED SKIRTS

Pleats are folds in the cloth (usually lengthwise) which are held in place by top-stitching, a seam, or the waistband. They are a design feature that adds fullness to the garment. Tucks are similar but smaller in size.

Pleats can be straight from top to bottom, or slightly deeper at the top to fit the skirt smoothly from hip to waist. (They can also be uneven in width as you learned on page 31.) They are usually planned to fit the width of the material, which is often striped, checked or plaid.

The fabric can be pleated first and then cut using a pattern, or the pattern can be slashed and spread to develop the pleats. To complete the altered pattern, fold in the pleats to cut seams, waist or hem.

A straight pleated skirt can be made from one or more even-width strips of fabric, and can be drafted from the measurements of length (plus hem) and width. (A gathered skirt can be made in the same way.) Work out the size, number and placement of the pleats in paper, then take careful measurements to determine how much fabric you will need. Plan seams to fall at the back of pleats where they will not show.

Pleats are classified according to the placement and number of folds they have.

Pleats can be made in many ways, either solid or in groups with spaces between them. They range in size from tiny knife-pleats to large box pleats.

Decide how long the skirt or pleated section will be. Take the measurement of the line the pleats will meet, whether it is the waistband or yoke or other line. Divide this measurement by the number of pleats to get the size of the pleats, or by the size of the pleats to get the number needed. A solid pleated skirt requires at least three times the circumference. Always allow several extra inches of fabric as a precaution in case of error. If the skirt needs to be pieced, plan these seams so that they are concealed under a pleat. Work out the pleats in paper as suggested earlier.

Pleats are easiest to make in a flat hemmed strip. Stitch the final seam after all the pleating is done. Carefully measure and mark the pleats with pins. Press fold lines, and then form the pleats. Pin to hold. Pin into place on skirt or waistband, adjusting pleats as necessary for an exact fit. Determine the location of remaining skirt seam. Pin and stitch. Cut off excess beyond seam allowance. Press. Pin and stitch to skirt.

Pleats are most successful in thin crisp fabric such as taffeta, silk, cotton or worsted. Decorative skirts for dolls can be made of wide ribbon (silk, moire, warp print or embroidered), or of wide lace. These materials do not need to be hemmed, and are beautiful when a heading is used. Cover the stitching with ribbon for added impact. Starch the lace if it is too limp to pleat.

Fig. 205.

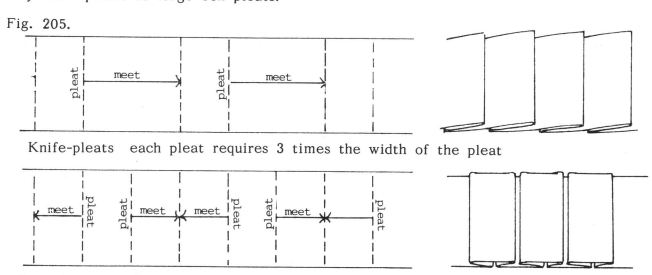

Knife-pleats   each pleat requires 3 times the width of the pleat

Box pleats   each pleat requires 3 times the width of the pleat

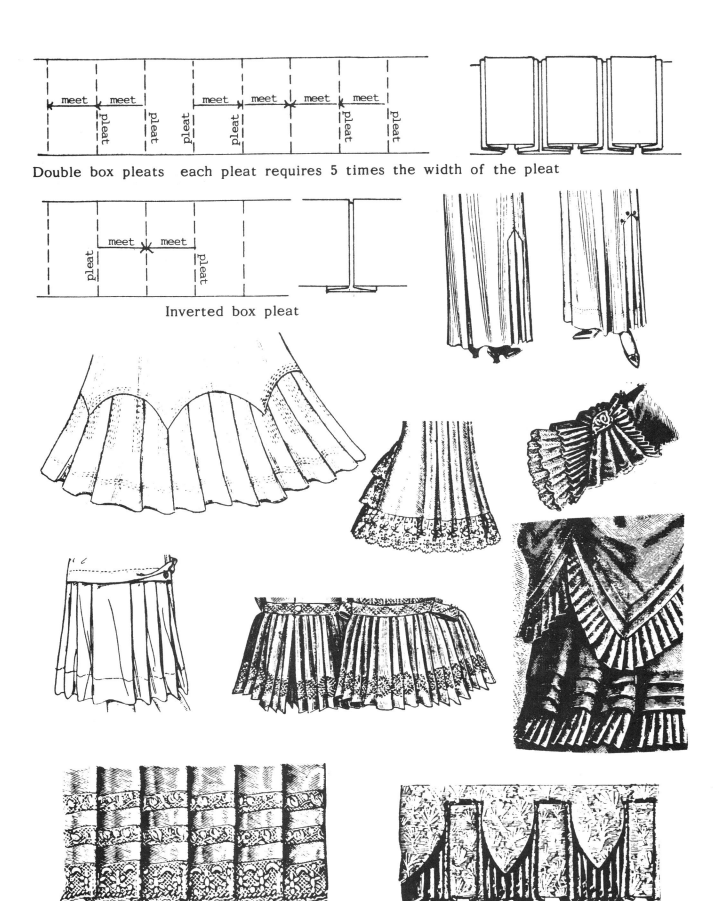

Double box pleats   each pleat requires 5 times the width of the pleat

Inverted box pleat

Fig. 206.

98

Reprinted from <u>Harper's</u>
<u>Bazar</u> 1916

<u>Delineator</u> 1901

Reprinted from
<u>Harper's Bazar</u>
1916

<u>Delineator</u> 1908

<u>Delineator</u> 1930

<u>Delineator</u> 1899

Fig. 207.

All illustrations from <u>Delineator Magazine</u>
used by permission of the Butterick Co., Inc.

13
Equipment

1. Clear plastic ruler marked in 1/8" lines.
2. French curve (various styles are available at art supply stores).
3. Right triangle.
4. Adjustable gauge used for sewing or knitting.
5. Tracing wheel and dressmaker's carbon paper.
6. Cellophane tape.
7. Scissors.
8. Pins and sewing supplies.
9. Padded surface or cardboard to pin the pattern to.
10. Paper.

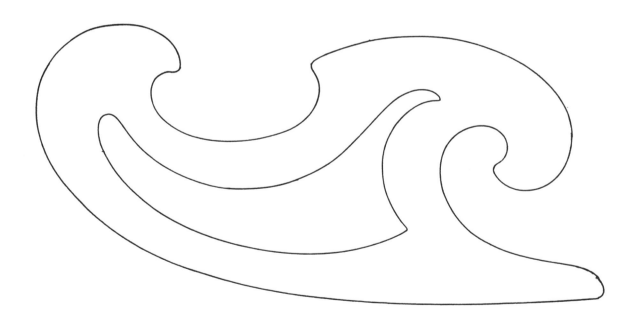

FRENCH CURVE

Photocopy and glue to cardboard or stiff plastic.
Cut out. Be sure edges are smooth.

14

Completing the Pattern

Flat pattern work should always be tested in fabric--either muslin or one that behaves in the same manner as that used for the finished garment. There is no substitute for seeing the design in fabric on the figure. If your pattern work was done in paper, transfer it to fabric, tracing all seam lines with a tracing wheel and dressmaker's carbon paper. Construct the garment and try it on the figure. Make needed changes, and transfer them back to the paper pattern. If you are working in muslin, the changes can be made directly in the fabric. Continue revising until you are satisfied with the design.

TO COMPLETE THE PATTERN:

1. **True all lines.**
   a) Perfect all lines using a ruler for straight lines and a French curve for the curved ones.
   b) Close all darts, pleats, tucks and extensions to perfect the seam lines. (On the wrong side, fold vertical darts toward the center, and horizontal darts down.)
   c) Check adjoining seams to be sure they match exactly. See that lines flow smoothly from one pattern piece to another.
   d) Convert designer's darts to dressmaker's darts. Curve fitting darts if you wish.

2. **Label all pieces.**
   Label each piece with name, size, pattern number or description and number of times it is to be cut. Asymmetrical designs should be labeled right and left so they can be cut face up on the right side of the fabric.

3. **Label construction lines.**
   Mark center front (CF), center back (CB), fold line ∴, grain line ←——→, darts and fold lines of hems. Show fold lines of pleats and the lines they are to meet using arrows to show the direction of the fold. Indicate the location of buttons, buttonholes, pockets or any other design details.

4. **Indicate assembling marks.**
   Mark notches, symbols to show where points meet, the exact location of gathers and ends of plackets. (Write an instruction sheet for information that cannot be noted on the pattern.)

5. **Add extensions and hems.**

6. **Make facings.**

7. **Add seam allowances.**

8. **Test the pattern.**

References

Pattern making

Erwin, Mabel D. Practical Dress Design. New York; The MacMillan Company, 1933, 1964.

Handford, Jack. Professional Patternmaking For Designers Of Women's Wear. Fullerton, California; Plycon Press, 1974.

Hollen, Norma R. Flat Pattern Methods. Minneapolis, Minnesota; Burgess Publishing Company, 1961, 1970.

Jaffe, Hilde and Relis, Nurie. Draping For Fashion Design. Reston, Virginia; Reston Publishing Company, 1973.

Margolis, Adele P. Make Your Own Patterns. New York; Doubleday & Company, 1985.

Sewing

Butterick, Vogue Sewing Book. New York; Harper & Row Publishers, Inc. 1982.

Iowa Home Economics Association. Unit Method of Clothing Construction. Ames, Iowa; The Iowa State University Press, 1965.

Art in clothing

Brockman, Helen. The Theory Of Fashion Design. New York, John Wiley & Sons, 1965.

McJimsey, Harriet T. Art In Clothing Selection. New York; Harper & Row Publishers, Inc., 1963.

Morton, Grace M. The Arts of Costume and Personal Appearance. New York; John Wiley & Sons. 1943, 1960.

Magazines (illustrations reprinted by permission)

Butterick patterns (from Delineator Magazine). New York; Butterick Company, Inc.

Harper's Bazar. New York; Harper's Bazaar.

Ladies' Home Journal. New York.

Vogue. New York; The Conde Nast Publications, Inc.

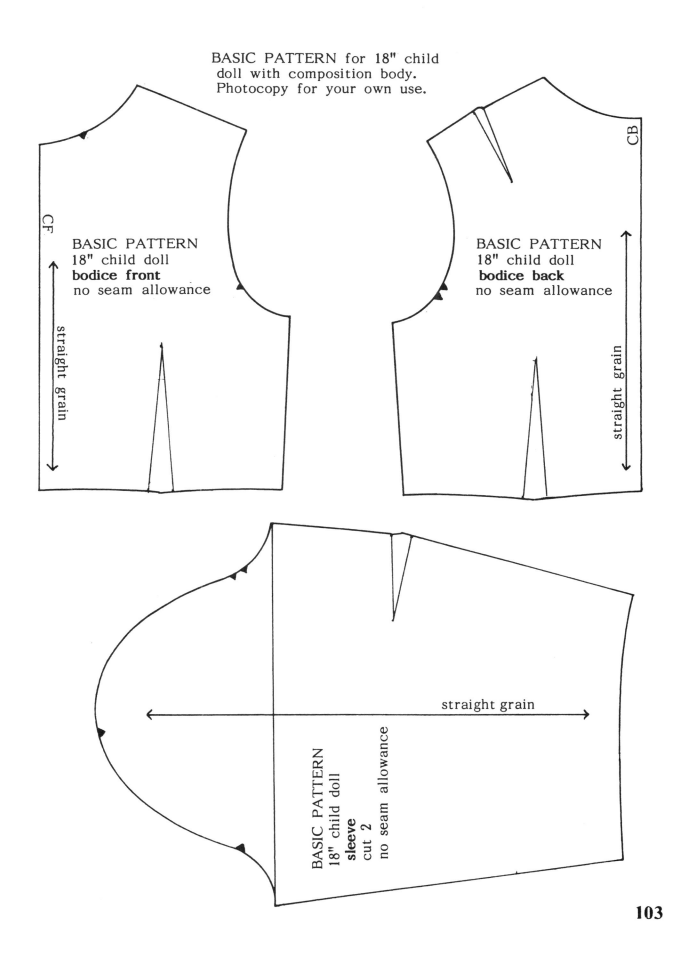

BASIC PATTERN for 18" child
doll with composition body.
Photocopy for your own use.

CF

BASIC PATTERN
18" child doll
bodice front
no seam allowance

straight grain

CB

BASIC PATTERN
18" child doll
bodice back
no seam allowance

straight grain

straight grain

BASIC PATTERN
18" child doll
sleeve
cut 2
no seam allowance

103

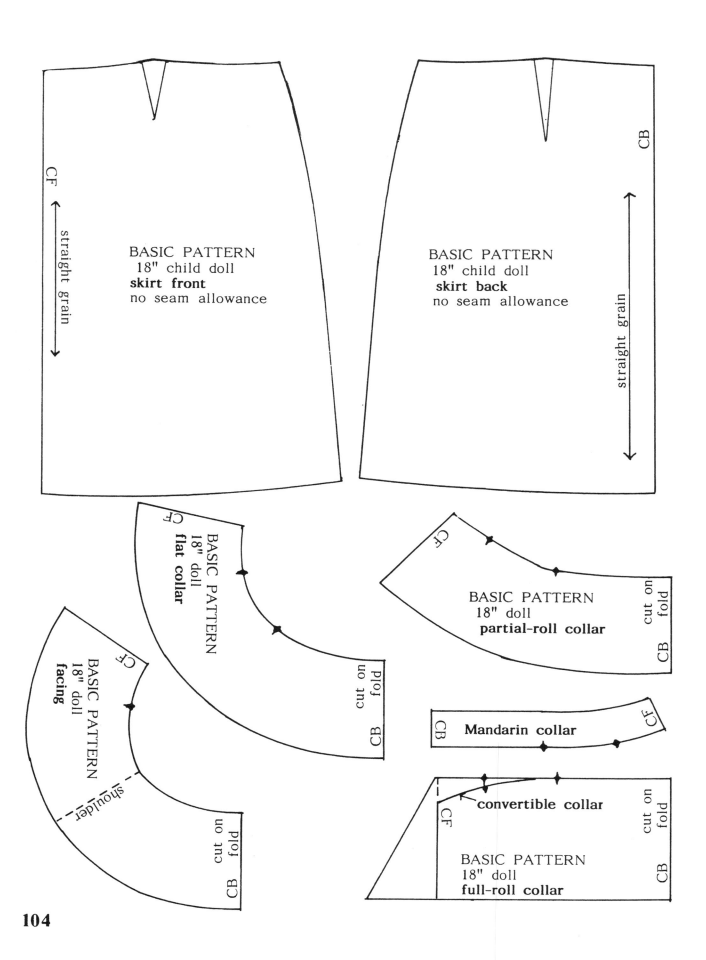

BASIC PATTERN
18" child doll
skirt front
no seam allowance

CF

straight grain

BASIC PATTERN
18" child doll
skirt back
no seam allowance

CB

straight grain

BASIC PATTERN
18" doll
flat collar

CF

cut on fold

CB

BASIC PATTERN
18" doll
partial-roll collar

CF

cut on fold

CB

BASIC PATTERN
18" doll
facing

CF

shoulder

cut on fold

CB

CB **Mandarin collar** CF

convertible collar

CF

BASIC PATTERN
18" doll
full-roll collar

cut on fold

CB

104